The LITTLE BOOK of COUNTRY MUSIC Wisdom

The LITTLE BOOK of COUNTRY MUSIC Wisdom

CHRIS PARTON

ILLUSTRATIONS BY NOAH ALBRECHT

GUILFORD, CONNECTICUT

An imprint of Globe Pequot

Distributed by NATIONAL BOOK NETWORK

Copyright © 2017 by Chris Parton
Illustrations by Noah Albrecht

British Library Cataloguing in Publication Information available

Library of Congress Cataloging-in-Publication Data
Names: Parton, Chris. | Albrecht, Noah illustrator.
Title: The little book of country music wisdom / Chris Parton ; illustrations by Noah Albrecht.
Description: Guilford, Connecticut : Lyons Press, [2017] | Includes bibliographical references.
Identifiers: LCCN 2017019006 (print) | LCCN 2017015185 (ebook) | ISBN 9781493029143 (e-book) | ISBN 9781493029136 (hardcover : alk. paper)
Subjects: LCSH: Country musicians—Quotations, maxims, etc.
Classification: LCC ML385 (print) | LCC ML385 .P246 2017 (ebook) | DDC 781.642—dc23
LC record available at https://lccn.loc.gov/2017019006

∞™
The paper used in this publication meets the minimum requirements of American National Standard for Information Sciences—Permanence of Paper for Printed Library Materials, ANSI/NISO Z39.48-1992.

Printed in the United States of America

FOR NAOMI

"AND NOW THREE OF THESE REMAIN: FAITH, HOPE, AND LOVE. BUT THE GREATEST OF THESE IS LOVE." —1 CORINTHIANS 13:13 NIV

contents

introduction

There's a lot to be learned from country stars and the simple, heartfelt songs they sing. But when the singing is over and real life begins, that's when the true, unvarnished wisdom of country music comes out.

It's found in Dolly Parton's childhood memories, filled with love in the face of poverty. It's in Reba McEntire's determination, Johnny Cash's moral compass, and Willie Nelson's jokes. It's in Carrie Underwood's dedication to health, Eric Church's fierce individuality, and even Luke Bryan's live-for-the-moment fun.

Filled with homespun hand-me-downs and first-hand experience, *The Little Book of Country Music Wisdom* is a pool of knowledge, guidance, and good humor, collected straight from the musings of America's modern day shade-tree philosophers—its country music stars.

chapter one
COUNTRY
for life

First and foremost, every country person (and as a result every country star) is proud of who they are, where they come from, and how they were raised. That means being honest, being strong in their convictions, and staying true to themselves.

"I FEEL STRONGLY ABOUT WHO I AM AND WHO I'M NOT, AND I'M COMFORTABLE WITH IT."

KACEY MUSGRAVES

Kacey Musgraves has been pressured to adopt a pop sound, but she has stuck to her guns and carved out her own place in country.

KNOWING WHO YOU ARE

"BEING A ROLE MODEL DOESN'T MEAN BEING PERFECT. IT MEANS BEING REAL AND TRUTHFUL AND HONEST."

KELSEA BALLERINI

Trying to be all things to all people might seem like good role modeling, but it's not sustainable. Country artist Kelsea Ballerini learned it's better to be yourself.

"WHEN I MADE MY FIRST TRIP TO NASHVILLE IN 1989, I WAS REALLY OUT OF SYNC WITH WHAT WAS GOING ON. I WAS SO OUT OF PLACE. BUT I COULDN'T CHANGE ALL OF MY MUSIC TO FIT WHAT WAS HAPPENING."

If the rock-inspired Aussie had altered his style during the cowboy-hats-and-Wranglers phase, Keith Urban would have never become one of country's biggest stars.

CHRIS JANSON

"EVERY TIME I'VE TRIED TO OVERTHINK SOMETHING IN MY LIFE, IT EITHER FAILED OR I WASN'T THAT PROUD OF IT."

Chris Janson's biggest success came when he decided to be himself with the hilariously infectious number one hit "Buy Me a Boat."

Dierks Bentley has scored mainstream radio hits, but he's also dared to think outside the box with a whole album of bluegrass-inspired music.

"I THINK I'VE CLAIMED THE RIGHT TO BE ANY VERSION OF ME THAT I WANT TO BE."

DIERKS BENTLEY

KNOWING WHO YOU ARE

It took Chase Bryant a few years to find himself, but his ultimate confidence made the waiting worthwhile.

"I FEEL LIKE YOU WILL SUCK AT BEING SOMEBODY ELSE, AND YOU *MIGHT* SUCK AT BEING YOURSELF AT FIRST, BUT AT SOME POINT YOU'RE GOING TO FIGURE IT OUT."

CHASE BRYANT

"I'D SAY MOST FOLKS ARE IN IT FOR THE RIGHT REASONS, BUT THERE ARE SOME SNAKES OUT THERE.... YOU'VE GOT TO WATCH OUT FOR YOUR BEST INTERESTS. YOU'VE GOT TO STICK TO YOUR GUNS AND YOUR MORALS AND WHAT MAKES YOU 'YOU,' BECAUSE IF YOU LOSE THAT, YOU KIND OF LOSE EVERYTHING."

SCOTTY McCREERY

Scotty McCreery was only sixteen when his career began, so there were a lot of experts trying to shape his decision making.

KNOWING WHO YOU ARE

18

> "I STUCK TO MY GUNS, AND I'M GLAD I DID. BECAUSE ALL OF THOSE PEOPLE THAT TRIED TO GET ME TO DO THAT, THEY'RE NOT EVEN IN THE BUSINESS ANYMORE. I'M STILL HERE AFTER TWENTY-SIX YEARS, WORKING."

MARK CHESNUTT

Mark Chesnutt once agreed to record an Aerosmith cover ("I Don't Want to Miss a Thing"). When his record label wanted more, he refused, keeping his integrity intact.

"IF YOU JUST PUT IT DOWN, BLACK AND WHITE, WHERE PEOPLE DON'T HAVE TO REALLY LISTEN TO HEAR WHAT YOU'RE SAYING, PEOPLE WILL SING ALONG WITH YOU. BUT IF YOU GO AROUND THE BUSH ABOUT EVERYTHING YOU'RE SAYING IN THEM LINES, THEY CAN'T SING WITH YOU."

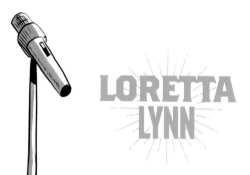

LORETTA LYNN

Country legend Loretta Lynn was explaining how to write a hit song, but her insight could be applied to everyday life.

"THOSE THINGS THAT YOU DON'T UNDERSTAND, THERE'S THIS EXTRA POWER TO THEM AND SOMETIMES YOU NEED TO DISMANTLE THAT IF IT'S A SCARY THING. I THINK THE MORE HONEST YOU CAN BE AND THE MORE UNCOMFORTABLE YOU FEEL AS YOU'RE EXPRESSING THOSE THINGS, GENERALLY MEANS IT HASN'T BEEN SAID ENOUGH. AND YOU SHOULD PROBABLY SAY IT MORE."

Country artist Cam earned a breakout hit in 2015 with "Burning House," a song rooted in bare honesty and real-life regrets.

MIRANDA LAMBERT

"I AM THIRTY-TWO YEARS OLD, AND WHAT LIFE HAS BROUGHT ME THE LAST YEAR—AND THERE'S GOOD AND BAD AND UGLY AND EVERYTHING IN BETWEEN—I THINK IT'S IMPORTANT TO JUST BE HONEST. THAT'S WHAT I'VE TRIED TO DO ABOVE EVERYTHING ELSE: JUST TELL THE TRUTH IN MY SOUL, BECAUSE THAT'S ALL WE HAVE."

The tabloids had a field day with Miranda Lambert and Blake Shelton's divorce, but instead of adding fuel to the fire by lashing out, she took the high road.

BILLY JOE SHAVER

"THE TRUTH USUALLY WINDS UP HURTING THE ONE THAT TELLS IT. I DON'T MIND STICKING MY NECK OUT. I'VE HAD AN AXE CLOSE TO MY NECK A TIME OR TWO."

Billy Joe Shaver is definitely known as a tough guy, but much of that reputation comes from his refusal to mince words.

Well-traveled stars like Tim McGraw are some of our strongest free-speech defenders. But as he points out, there's a difference between fact and opinion.

"EVERYONE SHOULD HAVE THEIR OWN OPINION AND BE ABLE TO VOICE IT—NO MATTER WHAT IT IS. OF COURSE, THAT DOES NOT MEAN YOUR OPINION IS ALWAYS RIGHT. BUT, YOU'RE CERTAINLY ENTITLED TO YOUR OPINION."

TIM McGRAW

It only took one trip to the Big Apple for Craig Morgan to change his preconceptions about it.

"AFTER I HAD THE EXPERIENCE OF GOING TO NEW YORK CITY FOR THE FIRST TIME AND REALIZING IT WAS NOTHING LIKE I'D EXPECTED, I REALIZED THAT OTHER PEOPLE HAD THE SAME PERCEPTIONS ABOUT ME."

CRAIG MORGAN

"YOU JUST DON'T KNOW WHAT PEOPLE ARE GOING THROUGH, AND I'VE HAD SO MANY SITUATIONS WHERE I'VE JUDGED SOMEONE BASED OFF WHAT I'VE HEARD OR FIRST IMPRESSIONS, AND THEN I GOT AROUND THEM AGAIN AND HAD A BETTER UNDERSTANDING OF THEM."

MICKEY GUYTON

Part of country artist Mickey Guyton's New Year's resolution for 2016 was to start giving more second chances.

EVERYBODY'S DIFFERENT

"WE'RE NOT ALL SUPPOSED TO BE ALIKE."

DOLLY PARTON

Dolly Parton has been truly unique ever since her mother sent her off to school in her "Coat of Many Colors."

ROSANNE CASH

"I SHOWED HIM AND HE NODDED. I SAID, 'YOU DON'T BELIEVE IN THIS, DO YOU?' HE SAID, 'NO, BUT I THINK YOU SHOULD FIND OUT EVERYTHING YOU CAN ABOUT IT.'"

When Rosanne Cash was nineteen her father, Johnny Cash, noticed her reading a book about astrology and surprised her with his tolerant nature.

"I'M FOR GROWING THINGS ORGANICALLY AND MAKING YOUR WAY AND BEING A SELF-MADE PERSON, AND I'M FOR ANY HUMAN DOING THAT."

Kacey Musgraves has sung about LGBT acceptance and casual marijuana use, but according to her, the only thing she's really an advocate for is being yourself.

In 2010, Chely Wright was the first main-stream country star to come out of the closet as a homosexual.

"I'M TRYING TO WORK ON THOSE THINGS AND TO USE MY VOICE TO MAKE SURE THAT EVERYONE OUT THERE IN AMERICA KNOWS, YOU DO LOVE A GAY PERSON. IT MAY NOT BE ME, BUT I PROMISE YOU, YOU HAVE A NEIGHBOR, A COWORKER, A NIECE. SO BE MINDFUL OF THE NEGATIVE THINGS YOU SAY ABOUT GAYS AND LESBIANS BECAUSE SOMEONE IS LISTENING."

CHELY WRIGHT

EVERYBODY'S DIFFERENT

Charley Pride became popular when segregation was still very real, and his talent helped change a lot of minds. "They didn't care if I was green," he liked to say about fans.

"A LOT OF PEOPLE WILL SAY, 'HOW DOES IT FEEL TO BE THE JACKIE ROBINSON OF COUNTRY MUSIC?' OR, 'HOW DOES IT FEEL TO BE THE FIRST COLORED COUNTRY SINGER?' 'HOW DOES IT FEEL TO BE THE FIRST NEGRO COUNTRY SINGER?'... I DON'T FEEL NO DIFFERENT."

"BACK WHEN I WAS ON *AMERICAN IDOL*, I WAS A BIT HEAVIER THAN I AM NOW. THAT WAS THE FIRST TIME I WAS EXPOSED TO THE PUBLIC TALKING ABOUT ME, SO IT WAS IMPOSSIBLE NOT TO LOOK ONLINE AND SEE WHAT THEY WERE SAYING. AND APPARENTLY, I WAS FAT. OF COURSE I WASN'T, BUT SOMETIMES WORDS PEOPLE CHOOSE ARE NOT THE NICEST. IT WAS A WAKE-UP CALL FOR ME IN THAT MAYBE I COULD STAND TO BE HEALTHIER. BUT IT WAS ALSO THE BEGINNING OF ME SAYING THAT IT SHOULDN'T MATTER WHAT OTHER PEOPLE SAY; IT'S ALL ABOUT HOW I FEEL."

CARRIE UNDERWOOD

Carrie Underwood has dealt with strangers passing judgment on her, and she's learned to turn the other cheek.

FORGETTING THE HATERS

"THERE WAS A TIME WHEN PEOPLE WERE LIKE 'YOU NEED TO PICK WHAT IT IS YOU WANT TO BE. DO YOU WANT TO BE A WRITER OR AN ARTIST?' I DECIDED I WAS JUST GOING TO DO WHAT I WANTED TO DO, AND I KNOW IT MIGHT NOT END EXACTLY HOW I THOUGHT, BUT I'M STILL GONNA GO AFTER ALL THOSE THINGS."

Singer-songwriter Cam learned to block out everything that conflicted with what she felt in her heart.

TYLER HUBBARD
OF FLORIDA GEORGIA LINE

"WE'LL TRY TO KEEP UP WITH WHAT'S HAPPENING IN THE NEWS WITH COUNTRY AND ALL THAT, BUT FOR THE MOST PART, MAN, WE'RE WORRIED ABOUT PLAYING SHOWS, WRITING SONGS AND GIVING OUR FANS WHAT THEY WANT, AND TRYING TO LIVE THE BEST WE CAN. SO FOR US, WE HEAR IT ALL, BUT WE DON'T REALLY LET IT AFFECT US VERY OFTEN."

Florida Georgia Line have helped push country music into exciting new territory, and they've dealt with some of the harshest criticism.

"A LOT OF TIMES I'LL JUST SIT THERE AND SMILE AT IT AND I'M LIKE, 'THIS IS PERFECT.' IF IT DOESN'T HIT A NERVE WITH PEOPLE, THEN IT'S ELEVATOR MUSIC."

Superstar Jason Aldean looks forward to people arguing about his music online. A strong reaction from fans—good or bad— is the goal.

To Kenny Chesney, the benefits of his
music outweigh the costs of his success.

"A LOT OF THINGS COME WITH SUCCESS—JEALOUSY, NEGATIVITY. BUT WITH SUCCESS ALSO COMES THE ABILITY TO MAKE A RECORD EVERY NOW AND THEN."

FORGETTING THE HATERS

Songwriter Dallas Davidson has learned that the best way to shut up naysayers is to achieve what they said can't be done.

"YOU HIT ME IN THE FACE, I'M GONNA HIT YOU BACK TWICE AS HARD. I LIKE TO USE THAT AS FUEL TO KEEP WORKING, BECAUSE IT'S EASY TO GET LAZY IN THIS BUSINESS.... I'M NOT AFTER ACCOLADES, BUT WHEN YOU DO WIN A SONGWRITER OF THE YEAR AWARD, IT'S BECAUSE YOU KICKED EVERYBODY'S *** THAT YEAR, AND THE REASON YOU KICKED EVERYBODY'S ASS IS BECAUSE YOU OUTWORKED THEM. IT NEVER GETS OLD."

DALLAS
DAVIDSON

"WHEN YOU HAVE SOMEBODY BAD-MOUTH YOU ON YOUR TWITTER PAGE, CALLING YOU THIS AND THAT, YOU LEARN TO GET IMMUNE TO IT, BUT SOMETIMES YOU'VE HAD ENOUGH AND YOU'LL POP OFF AT THEM. NEXT THING YOU KNOW, ALL MY FANS ARE ABSOLUTELY CRUSHING THEM, AND I FEEL BAD THAT I SHOULD HAVE JUST LET IT BE."

LUKE BRYAN

Luke Bryan knows the peace of mind that comes by taking the high road is better than the guilt of slipping down to the level of his detractors.

FORGETTING THE HATERS

"ONE NIGHT MY TOUR MANAGER SAID 'GOOD THINGS HAPPEN TO GOOD PEOPLE,' AND I WAS LIKE '... YEAH.' BUT IT BOTHERED ME AND I COULDN'T SLEEP—LIKE 'SOMETHING'S WRONG WITH THIS QUOTE,' YOU KNOW? AND I TOLD MYSELF 'GOOD THINGS HAPPEN TO GOOD PEOPLE, WHEN YOU'RE GOOD TO PEOPLE.' I THINK THAT'S BEEN THE BIGGEST LIFE LESSON OF BEING ON THE ROAD: TREAT EVERYONE LIKE THEY'RE ONE OF YOURS."

CHASE BRYANT

Going a step beyond "taking the high road," Chase Bryant discovered something even more powerful—treating others (even the mean ones) how you'd like to be treated.

SIX WORST
COUNTRY MUSIC
feuds

TRAVIS TRITT VS. BILLY RAY CYRUS
Billy Ray Cyrus had the hottest single out there in 1992—
the danceable hit "Achy Breaky Heart"—but not everyone
liked it. Fellow singer Travis Tritt famously declared that the
song and its line-dancing video were turning country into an
"***-wiggling contest."

ZAC BROWN VS. LUKE BRYAN AND JASON ALDEAN
Zac Brown did not have much love for Luke Bryan's "That's
My Kind of Night" in 2013, calling it the worst song he had
ever heard. Bryan took the high road and didn't respond, but
friends like Jason Aldean did, writing "Trust me when I tell
you that nobody gives a **** what you think" on Instagram.

KRISTEN HALL VS. SUGARLAND
Country duo Sugarland was actually a trio when it started
out, but in 2005—just as the band hit the big time—founding member Kristen Hall left the group. Rumors swirled
that she was pushed out, and in 2008 she filed a $14 million
lawsuit over profits from their debut album. The lawsuit was

settled out of court, but the reason for her departure was never fully explained.

FAITH HILL VS. CARRIE UNDERWOOD

The 2006 CMA Awards turned into a controversy when superstar Faith Hill appeared outraged over losing the Female Vocalist of the Year award to then-newcomer Carrie Underwood. Both sides went into damage-control mode, with Hill saying she was just goofing around and Underwood saying the two had talked and everything was fine. Some fans still believe Hill's reaction was genuine.

BLAKE SHELTON VS. RAY PRICE

In response to some negativity aimed at his lighthearted country hits in 2013, Blake Shelton was quoted saying, "Nobody wants to listen to their grandpa's music" and calling country purists "old farts" and "jackasses." Country legend Ray Price took offense, ripping into Shelton and telling him to "check back in sixty-three years" to see how his music holds up. Shelton apologized.

TOBY KEITH VS. THE DIXIE CHICKS

When the Dixie Chicks' Natalie Maines made her infamous comment that she was ashamed President George W. Bush was from Texas (owing to America's entry into the Iraq War in 2003), it wasn't just fans who were outraged. Public comments and even snide T-shirts were tossed between her and Toby Keith, and the foes have never reconciled.

chapter two

IT'S GOOD
to be home

Home and family are two important
pillars in any country life, and without
one, the other doesn't exist. Country stars
are always inspired by where they came
from and how they were raised, and they
feel pretty strongly about carrying their
traditions on.

Blake Shelton films in the big city of Los Angeles for *The Voice*, but he goes back to his Oklahoma farm whenever possible.

"AS SOON AS WE'RE DONE ON WEDNESDAYS, MY *** IS ON THE PLANE. IT'S JUST LIKE PLUGGING IN YOUR PHONE. I GET IN MY TRUCK, I SEE THE FIELDS, SEE THE COWS."

BLAKE SHELTON

THERE'S NO PLACE LIKE HOME

None of his country-star fun can compare
to Joe Nichols's feeling of being home
with his wife and daughters.

"EVERY TIME I COME HOME I FEEL LIKE I'M SURROUNDED BY JOY AND I THINK THAT'S WHAT HAVING A FAMILY IS ALL ABOUT."

"OF ALL MY BUDDIES, I WAS THE ONE KID WHO NEVER WANTED TO MOVE AWAY FROM HOME, AND I'M THE ONLY ONE WHO ENDED UP DOING IT.... NASHVILLE WAS GREAT TO ME. I HAVE A LOT OF GREAT FRIENDS THERE AND I CAN'T COMPLAIN, BUT IT JUST WASN'T HOME. ALL MY FAMILY ARE STILL HERE IN ARKANSAS.... IT WAS IMPORTANT FOR ME THAT MY KIDS GREW UP GETTING TO SEE THEIR GRANDPARENTS."

JUSTIN MOORE

After Justin Moore established himself as a hit maker, he moved his family back to his hometown of Poyen, Arkansas, population 300.

"I LOVE IT ALL AND I LOVE THE FANS, BUT OF COURSE HOME IS HOME."

DOLLY PARTON

Dolly Parton has toured from New York to New Zealand, but there's a special feeling that comes from being "home."

"ANY TIME ANY SIGNIFICANT THING HAP-PENS IN YOUR LIFE, THE ONE PLACE THAT YOU SUBCONSCIOUSLY ALWAYS TURN [IS YOUR] HOMETOWN. I WOULD JUST WANT TO GO HOME FOR TWO OR THREE DAYS, AND WHATEVER I WAS GOING THROUGH ... WOULD DISAPPEAR."

Powerhouse singer David Nail has bat-tled publicly with depression and anxiety, but he could always turn home for relief.

ERIC CHURCH

"THERE'S A LOT OF GHOSTS THERE. I CAN'T TELL YOU THE NUMBER OF TIMES TODAY I COULD SEE MY GRANDFATHER EITHER STANDIN' ON THE BANK, OR ON THE PORCH OF THE HOUSE, BY THE BARN—ALL THESE DIFFERENT PLACES. IT WAS A LITTLE HAUNTING IN A WAY, BUT I THINK IT'S OKAY. I THINK THAT'S WHAT MAKES IT WHAT IT IS."

When Eric Church visited the mountainside cabin where his grandfather lived in North Carolina, he realized that memories of home are what mold a person into who they are.

After more than eighty years of practice,
country legend Willie Nelson has learned
to love the family he has.

"THEY SAY THE ONLY NORMAL FAMILY IS THE ONE YOU DON'T REALLY KNOW."

WILLIE
NELSON

Across cultures, races, and everything else,
Kellie Pickler sees what unites us.

"EVERY FAMILY, I FEEL LIKE WE ALL HAVE A
LOT MORE IN COMMON THAN WE MAY GIVE
CREDIT TO."

KELLIE
PICKLER

"I HAD TO LEARN THE HARD WAY THAT FAMILY TIME IS WAY MORE IMPORTANT THAN YOUR CAREER. I HAVE PUT A LOT INTO MY CAREER, BUT I WANT TO START PUTTING MORE INTO MY FAMILY AND KNOW THAT THEY ARE PROUD."

COLE SWINDELL

Cole Swindell's father died tragically in 2013, just as the young singer's career was taking off. The loss inspired the hit song "You Should Be Here."

"IT IS MY TRUE BELIEF THAT IF YOU'RE LUCKY ENOUGH TO HAVE A GOOD MOTHER, THAT IS THE GREATEST GIFT THAT YOU WILL EVER KNOW."

DOLLY PARTON

Dolly Parton grew up in a tiny shack in the Appalachian Mountains of Tennessee with eleven brothers and sisters.

KELSEA BALLERINI

"MY MOM IS A ROCK STAR. SHE'S SUPER COOL AND SUPER GROUNDED. SHE'LL BE THE FIRST ONE TO SAY 'KELSEA, THAT DRESS IS TOO SHORT, GO CHANGE,' OR 'KELSEA, THAT SONG IS NOT WHO YOU ARE, DON'T SING THAT.' SHE HELPS ME STAY MY PATH, BUT SHE'S ALSO VERY DRIVEN AND SAYS 'YOU CAN DO IT. YOU GOT IT.'"

Kelsea Ballerini has discovered the truth in Dolly Parton's "good mother" wisdom.

KEITH URBAN

"[MY DAD] WAS INTO IT, AND I WANTED HIS APPROVAL. I FEEL VERY SURE IF HE'D BEEN INTO AFRICAN MUSIC, I'D BE LIVING IN ZIMBABWE, HAVING THE SAME TALK ABOUT 'WOW, THEY MUST HAVE THOUGHT YOU WERE STRANGE WHEN YOU GOT TO THIS TOWN.'"

Keith Urban says his dad was the driving force behind his picking up country music.

TJ and John Osborne of Brothers Osborne take full advantage of their unbreakable sibling bond.

"WE CAN BE BRUTALLY HONEST AND JUST CUT THROUGH THE BULL****. WITH OTHER PEOPLE YOU KIND OF HAVE TO BE CAREFUL NOT TO RUFFLE ANY FEATHERS.... WE GET IT OVER WITH AND WE GET TO MOVE ON, SO IT KEEPS IT VERY EFFICIENT."

TJ OSBORNE
OF BROTHERS OSBORNE

FAMILY FIRST

In 1968, with the deal for his TV variety show in the works, Cash wanted to remind himself where his true focus should be.

"THE BIGGEST DEAL YOU'VE GOT IS YOUR FAMILY AND HOME. YOU'D BETTER HANG WITH GOD IF YOU WANT THE OTHER DEALS TO WORK OUT."

JOHNNY CASH

"EVERY DAY WHEN I'M HOME, ME AND CAROLINE GET IN BED AROUND 10 P.M., AND IT LOOKS LIKE WE HAVE DONE A TRIATHLON.... IT CHALLENGES EVERY DAY AND YOU LEARN AND LEARN."

LUKE BRYAN

Luke Bryan thought he knew what a long day was, but that was before he and wife Caroline started raising kids.

"WHEN I WROTE AND RECORDED *THAT GIRL*, I HAD A FIVE-MONTH-OLD SON. THAT, IN AND OF ITSELF, IS SUCH A TRANSFORMATIVE PROCESS. THERE'S A BIG VEIL THE FIRST COUPLE OF YEARS, ESPECIALLY FOR NEW MOTHERS, OF SLEEP DEPRIVATION AND IDENTITY CRISIS, AT LEAST FOR ME."

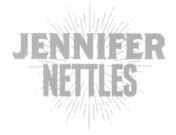

JENNIFER NETTLES

Solo artist and Sugarland member Jennifer Nettles's message for first-time moms? "It's OK to feel overwhelmed."

KEIFER THOMPSON
OF THOMPSON SQUARE

"THE MOMENT THEY PUT HIM INTO MY ARMS, I WAS LIKE, 'THIS IS REAL.' I NEVER REALLY FELT MATURE. I ALWAYS FELT LIKE THE KID IN THE ROOM, YOU KNOW? AND, I DON'T ANYMORE. RIGHT THERE, IT ALL SWITCHED FOR ME."

Keifer and Shawna Thompson of Thompson Square found a whole new sense of maturity and purpose.

THE TOUGHEST JOB

60

WILLIE NELSON

"MY GREATEST JOY IS SEEING ALL MY KIDS ONSTAGE SINGING TOGETHER. IT'S REALLY HARD TO BEAT THAT DNA HARMONY SOUND. I AM REALLY HAPPY WHEN THEY ARE ALL OUT THERE SINGING INDIVIDUALLY, BUT KNOCKED OUT WHEN THEY ARE STANDING AT THE MICROPHONE RIGHT NEXT TO ME, SINGING THEIR HEARTS OUT TOGETHER."

When Willie Nelson's kids come together, the feeling of pride can be joyously overwhelming.

Kenny Rogers and wife Wanda welcomed twin boys in 2004 when Rogers was sixty-five years old.

"I DON'T THINK HE EVER SAW BUT TWO OF MY SHOWS. WHEN I WAS PLAYING IN JAZZ GROUPS IN TEXAS, HE NEVER CAME. AND SUBLIMINALLY, THAT BOTHERED ME.... I KNOW THIS SOUNDS TERRIBLE, BUT I REALLY WANT TO BE THE FATHER TO MY TWIN BOYS THAT MY FATHER WASN'T TO ME."

KENNY ROGERS

THE TOUGHEST JOB

Country icon Tanya Tucker's kids have gotten into the family business— country music.

"THEY'VE SEEN A LOT FROM ME BEING ON THE ROAD AND GROWING UP ON THE ROAD, AND I CAN ONLY HOPE IT HELPS THEM GET AROUND A COUPLE OF THOSE HOLES I'VE FALLEN IN. MAYBE THEY CAN STEP AROUND A COUPLE OF THEM, AND HOPEFULLY I'VE SHOWED THEM THAT—THE BEHIND THE SCENES OF EVERYTHING AND THE WAY THINGS REALLY ARE."

TANYA TUCKER

"YOU THINK YOU KNOW WHAT LOVE IS, BUT YOU DON'T REALLY UNTIL YOU MEET THIS LITTLE PERSON."

CHARLES KELLEY
OF LADY ANTEBELLUM

Lady Antebellum's Charles Kelley and his wife Cassie had their first child in 2016.

THE TOUGHEST JOB

"I'M NOT THAT TOUGH. I MEAN, I TRY TO ACT LIKE I AM, BUT I JUST WANT THEM TO BE HAPPY."

TIM MCGRAW

Having raised three daughters, country icon Tim McGraw has admitted that they have him wrapped around their fingers.

COUNTRY STAR HOMES
worth visiting

GEORGE JONES

The late George Jones lived in Franklin, Tennessee, in a nearly 10,000-square-foot mansion on twenty-five acres that featured four bedrooms, eight bathrooms, a seven-car garage, and two barns. He called it the Country Gold Estate, and it sold in 2015 for $1.98 million.

BARBARA MANDRELL

Country fans can actually go inside Barbara Mandrell's former home, the Mansion at Fontanel. Located just outside Nashville, the 33,000-square-foot log cabin has two kitchens, thirteen bathrooms, five fireplaces, and even an indoor shooting range.

ALAN JACKSON

When Alan Jackson put his massive Sweetbriar Estate on the market in 2009, he listed it for a whopping $38 million. With its own lake and boathouse and sitting on 135 acres in Franklin, Tennessee, the property is a popular spot for drive-by sightseeing.

JOHN RICH

John Rich of Big & Rich opted to build his home right in the heart of Music City. Called Mt. Richmore, the ultramodern mansion is located on a hill facing downtown Nashville and features interesting amenities like a full-scale nightclub and rooftop lawn.

TAYLOR SWIFT

Taylor Swift also likes living inside Nashville's city limits and bought a penthouse condo for just shy of $2 million in 2009. The two-story, 4,000-square-foot space sits on top of the Adelicia condo building and features a human-size birdcage filled with pillows.

JOHNNY CASH

Johnny Cash's famous lakeside cabin sadly burned down in 2007, but fans can still get a glimpse of what it was like inside from the Johnny Cash Museum in Nashville. There a whole wall and mantel from the Cash home have been reassembled and decorated with family mementos.

chapter three
FAITH
never fails

Country folks have a sense of spirituality that is at the center of their daily lives. Most have grown up in the church, and for them a personal relationship with God's word is a roadmap to a meaningful and happy life.

"I'M A PRIVATE GUY, AND YOU DON'T WANT TO BE OUT THERE PREACHING TO PEOPLE. BUT FAITH LEADS YOU IN THE DECISIONS YOU MAKE. YOU DON'T ALWAYS PICK THE RIGHT PATH, BUT IT'S THERE IN YOUR CONSCIENCE."

Whether he talks about it or not, faith is behind everything Tim McGraw does—even when his choices turn out to be mistakes.

STICK TO THE PLAN

REBA MCENTIRE

"I HAVE BEEN PUT ON THIS EARTH FOR A REASON, AND I LISTEN TO GOD DAILY ON WHAT HE WANTS ME TO DO NEXT. PEOPLE WILL SAY, 'WELL, WHATCHA GONNA DO NEXT?' I SAY, 'I HAVE NO IDEA, GOD HASN'T TOLD ME YET.' ... I GIVE HIM ALL THE CREDIT BECAUSE I SURE DIDN'T THINK IT UP."

Reba McEntire lets God show her the way forward.

Someone higher must've been pulling the strings when Tom T. Hall decided not to trash a song he had just written called "Little Bitty."

"ALAN JACKSON HEARD IT, AND I ASKED HIM, 'WHAT DO YOU THINK OF THIS SONG?' AND HE SAID, 'I THINK IT'S A LITTLE BITTY HIT,' AND HE RECORDED IT AND MADE IT ONE. BUT THAT THING STAYED IN MY DRAWER FOR TWO YEARS AFTER I WROTE IT, SO IT'S A DANGEROUS BUSINESS.... I THINK I HAD THE OPTION OF THROWING ALL THAT STUFF IN A WASTEBASKET OR PUTTING IT IN A DRAWER, AND I DECIDED TO PUT IT IN A DRAWER."

TOM T. HALL

STICK TO THE PLAN

Collin Raye has learned to seize the good times with a smile and a "Thank you" to the man upstairs.

"I JUST WAIT AND SEE WHAT GOD PUSHES MY WAY, BUT THERE'S ALWAYS SOMETHING. IT'S NOT LIKE WE GO OUT AND SEEK THESE THINGS OUT. ALL OF A SUDDEN, YOU GET AN E-MAIL OR A CALL, 'HEY, DO YOU WANT TO DO THIS MOVIE?' WHEN IT FITS LIKE THAT, I GO, 'THANK YOU. THANK YOU, LORD. THAT WAS A GIFT FROM YOU.'"

COLLIN RAYE

"I WENT THROUGH THIRTY DAYS OF READING THE BIBLE, KEEPING MY MIND OFF OF ANYTHING ELSE, AND THE BIBLE WAS ONE OF THE BOOKS THAT I REALLY BELIEVED IN BUT NEVER LIVED OR READ LIKE I SHOULD HAVE UNTIL I WAS IN THE HOSPITAL. I SAW A DIFFERENT LIFE. I DIDN'T KNOW THERE WAS A WAY BACK."

GEORGE JONES

Country legend George Jones almost lost his life to alcoholism, but he was saved by a renewed faith and his wife Nancy's care.

STICK TO THE PLAN

"I REALLY HAVE NO ANXIETY ABOUT CONTROLLING MY OWN LIFE. SOMEHOW I JUST SLIPPED INTO IT AND IT'S WORKED. IT'S NOT UP TO ME—OR YOU. I FEEL VERY LUCKY THAT [LIFE]'S LASTED SO LONG BECAUSE I'VE DONE SO MANY THINGS THAT COULD HAVE KNOCKED ME OUT OF IT. BUT SOMEHOW I JUST ALWAYS HAVE THE FEELING THAT HE KNOWS WHAT HE'S DOING. IT'S BEEN GOOD SO FAR, AND IT'LL PROBABLY CONTINUE TO BE."

KRIS KRISTOFFERSON

Kris Kristofferson has taken stock and become grateful that his life was happy in spite of his mistakes.

KELSEA
BALLERINI

"I REALIZED THAT GRACE HAS BEEN A REAL THEME THROUGHOUT MY LIFE. IT'S ONE OF THE BIGGEST GIFTS TO GIVE, AND GET."

Kelsea Ballerini has a tattoo on her arm that reads "How sweet the sound" from "Amazing Grace."

THE GOLDEN RULE

NEAL McCOY

"IF YOU'LL PUT ON A GREAT SHOW AND BE NICE TO PEOPLE, YOU CAN CONTINUE TO WORK IN THIS BUSINESS.... WHEN WE HAD OUR SUCCESS, MUSIC-WISE, WE WERE GRACIOUS. PEOPLE WOULD BRING US BACK. SOME OF THESE PLACES YOU'LL PLAY TWO, THREE, FOUR, TEN TIMES. THESE PEOPLE WILL REMEMBER. THAT'S WHAT WE LEARNED."

Neal McCoy tries to treat everyone with respect and gratitude, the key—he believes—to doing well in the long run.

Carrie Underwood and husband Mike Fisher have decided to be very proactive when it comes to encouraging compassion in their son, Isaiah.

"MIKE AND I TALK ABOUT TEACHING HIM HOW TO APPROACH EVERYBODY IN A LOVING WAY, EVEN IF THEY'RE NOT THE SAME, AND TO TRY TO SAY, 'YOU KNOW WHAT? GOD LOVES THEM, SO IT SHOULD BE MY JOB TO DO MY BEST TO LOVE THEM AS WELL.'"

CARRIE UNDERWOOD

Willie Nelson believes doing right and sharing what you have is good for your conscience and your pocketbook.

"THE BIBLE SAYS WHATEVER YOU GIVE AWAY YOU GET BACK TEN TIMES OVER. DO THE MATH; IT'S A NO-BRAINER."

WILLIE NELSON

"MY MAMA ALWAYS TAUGHT ME THAT GOOD THINGS COME FROM ADVERSITY IF WE PUT OUR FAITH IN THE LORD. WE COULDN'T SEE MUCH GOOD IN THE FLOODWATERS WHEN THEY WERE CAUSING US TO LEAVE HOME. BUT WHEN THE WATER WENT DOWN, WE FOUND THAT IT HAD WASHED A LOAD OF RICH BLACK BOTTOM DIRT ACROSS OUR LAND. THE FOLLOWING YEAR WE HAD THE BEST CROP WE'D EVER HAD."

JOHNNY CASH

Johnny Cash learned early on that there are seasons in life, and even the toughest season can give us something we really need.

THE BIGGER PICTURE

80

"LOVE IS GOD, AND GOD IS LOVE, END OF STORY."

To hear Willie Nelson explain it, applying faith to real life isn't so complicated.

KENNY CHESNEY

"THERE'S THINGS ABOUT RELIGION THAT I DON'T NECESSARILY AGREE WITH OR UNDERSTAND, BUT I'M A BIG BELIEVER IN SPIRITUALITY—I'VE SEEN SONGS CHANGE PEOPLE."

To Kenny Chesney, the transformative power of music proves that there's more to life than meets the eye.

THE BIGGER PICTURE

TY HERNDON

"I SIT ON THE TAILGATE OF MY PICKUP TRUCK, AND I MEDITATE, AND I TALK TO GOD. THAT'S REALLY ALL I NEED TO KNOW. I HAVE A CONNECTION TO SOMETHING BIGGER THAN MYSELF, AND NO ONE'S GOING TO TELL ME THAT I CAN'T HAVE IT. WE GET TO CHOOSE WHO WE LOVE, AND THAT INCLUDES GOD, AND HE LOVES US BACK."

Ty Herndon's personal relationship with God led him to finally come out of the closet as a gay man in 2014.

After the passing of his brother, sister, and her husband, Luke Bryan and his wife Caroline now raise their nieces and nephews.

"THE LOSSES GAVE ME SUCH A DEEP PERSPECTIVE OF LIFE—HOW TOUGH IT CAN GET AT ANY SECOND. YOU QUESTION IT EVERY DAY, BUT YOU HAVE TO REVERT BACK TO YOUR FAITH IN GOD'S PLAN."

LUKE BRYAN

Even powerhouse vocalists like Wynonna feel weak sometimes, but with God by her side she never feels alone.

"AFTER MY FATHER DIED—I NEVER MET HIM—I WENT THROUGH A PERIOD OF NOT BEING REALLY SURE WHAT TO DO NEXT. THERE ARE TIMES IN YOUR LIFE WHEN YOU KNOW HOW TO WORK, HOW TO GET UP IN THE MORNING, BUT WHEN THE QUIET STILLNESS OF THE NIGHT COMES, YOU KIND OF SIT THERE AND GO, 'WELL, IS THIS ALL THAT IT'S ABOUT?' AND IN A FLASH I REALIZED, THOUGH I NEVER GOT TO MEET MY EARTHLY FATHER, I WILL MEET MY HEAVENLY FATHER, AND I BELIEVE THAT."

WYNONNA

Johnny Cash SEES THE LIGHT

After his divorce and at the height of his drug abuse, country icon Johnny Cash decided to end it all.

Strung out and feeling alone, he climbed into Nickajack Cave in southeastern Tennessee intending to never come out, just like some unfortunate explorers had before. Writing in his second autobiography, Cash says he walked for hours into the cavern until his flashlight gave out and then laid down to die—but instead, something else happened.

"The absolute lack of light was appropriate," he wrote. "For at that moment I was as far from God as I have ever been. My separation from Him, the deepest and most ravaging of the various kinds of loneliness I'd felt over the years, seemed finally complete."

In his shame, Cash tried to get as far away from God as he could. But laying there in the darkness he experienced a life-changing revelation: God hadn't abandoned him, even after this. He emerged a different man.

"There in the Nickajack Cave I became conscious of a very clear, simple idea," wrote the weary star. "I was going to die at God's time, not mine. I hadn't prayed over my decision to seek death in the cave, but that hadn't stopped God from intervening."

chapter four
GROWING UP
country

Where and how a child grows up has a huge impact on who they become, and being raised country often inspires a unique point of view, gives them a long list of skills, and instills a strong sense of right and wrong.

"I LOVE BEING FROM THE COUNTRY, AND I LOVE BRINGING UP OLIVIA AND LUKE IN THE SAME PLACE I WAS RAISED. I THINK THERE IS A CERTAIN SOMETHING ABOUT FOLKS IN THE COUNTRY. I THINK YOU LEARN HOW TO MAKE THE BEST OF WHAT YOU HAVE, AND THAT MAY NOT ALWAYS BE A LOT. I ALSO THINK YOU LEARN TO 'COWBOY UP' AND PICK YOURSELF UP WHEN YOU GET BUCKED OFF."

CHARLIE DANIELS

Some country stars could choose to raise their children anywhere, but many—like Charlie Daniels—hope to give their kids something only a childhood in the country can.

"WELL, AS I ALWAYS SAY, 'WHEREVER YOU'RE FROM, IT'S A SMALL TOWN.'"

BRANDY CLARK

To Brandy Clark, you can find small-town connections between people everywhere.

"I FEEL LIKE, ESPECIALLY IF YOU COME FROM A SMALL TOWN, THERE ARE CERTAIN VALUES THAT ARE INHERENT, FEARS AND INSECURITIES THAT WE ALL HAVE, AND THAT WAS ME. I WAS THAT KID—I'D GO OUT IN THE MIDDLE OF THE BACKYARD AT MY GRANDMA'S HOUSE AND STARE UP AT THE SKY AND WONDER IF THERE WAS ANYTHING OUT THERE BEYOND MY COUNTY LINE."

Being from the country was peaceful and idyllic, but also inspired Kenny Chesney's restless spirit and desire to explore the world.

ALAN JACKSON

"EVEN THOUGH DENISE AND I HAVE MADE A LOT OF MONEY, WE'RE NOT REAL SOCIALITES. WE DON'T HAVE BIG PARTIES. WE JUST HAVE THE SAME OLD CORNBREAD AND PEAS I DID WHEN I WAS GROWING UP."

Even with a giant mansion and dozens of cars, trucks, boats, and more, Alan Jackson is country-kid modest.

Something about the small-town lifestyle pulled Justin Moore back.

"I ALWAYS KNEW I LOVED IT THERE. I WAS ONE OF THE GUYS WHO NEVER WANTED TO LEAVE. THERE ARE A LOT OF PEOPLE WHO ARE LIKE, 'I CAN'T WAIT TO GET THE HECK OUT OF DODGE.' I NEVER WANTED THAT. BUT IN ORDER TO DO WHAT I DO, IT WAS ABSOLUTELY NECESSARY. I MISSED IT FROM DAY ONE."

JUSTIN MOORE

Country legend Loretta Lynn believes the world would be a better place with more country values and skills.

"THE COUNTRY IS MAKING A BIG MISTAKE NOT TEACHING KIDS TO COOK AND RAISE A GARDEN AND BUILD FIRES."

LORETTA LYNN

"MY DAD TAUGHT ME HOW TO BE A MAN. HE TAUGHT ME HOW TO STICK UP FOR MYSELF. IF YOU COME HOME AND SOMEONE'S BEEN PICK-ING ON YOU AT SCHOOL, HE'D SAY, 'KNOCK HIS TEETH OUT AND HE'LL LEAVE YOU ALONE.'"

Jason Aldean learned to stand tall and fight back at an early age.

"I DON'T START FIGHTS, BUT I TRY REALLY HARD TO FINISH THEM."

BILLY JOE SHAVER

Billy Joe Shaver once shot a knife-wielding man in the face (the man lived, and Shaver was acquitted by reason of self-defense).

WILLIE NELSON

"I'VE BEEN BEATEN UP A FEW TIMES, AND I NEVER LEARNED TO LIKE IT. IF I CAN SCARE YOU OFF WITH BIG TALK, I'LL TRY THAT FIRST. HIDE GROWS BACK, BUT GOOD CLOTHES DON'T."

Willie Nelson's philosophy on fighting is a bit different—he's like a dog with a whole lot of bark but not much bite.

GETTING TOUGH

MIRANDA LAMBERT

"I FEEL LIKE I GOT OVER THE HUMP OF TRYING TO BE LIKE, 'I HAVE A CHIP ON MY SHOULDER, I'M STRONG ALL THE TIME,' YOU KNOW? BECAUSE NO ONE IS."

After her divorce from Blake Shelton, Miranda Lambert discovered that even the toughest people need to break down and cry once in a while.

We all go through trials and tribulations, but Kip Moore knows that some of us are tougher than others.

"MY GRANDPARENTS WERE IN THE MILITARY, FOUGHT WARS, AND I'VE SEEN THE BATTLE THAT THEY GO THROUGH, JUST THE HORROR OF REMEMBERING THINGS. WHEN I START TO THINK THAT I'M HALFWAY TOUGH, I REALIZE HOW I'M NOT ONE BIT WHEN I TALK TO SOLDIERS WHEN I'M OUT AND REALIZE THE THINGS THAT THEY GO THROUGH."

KIP MOORE

GETTING TOUGH

For Trace Adkins, a former oil rig worker and football player, scars are proof of how much life a person has lived.

"MY TOUGHNESS HAS BEEN DOCUMENTED. I HAVE THE SCARS AND SURGERIES TO PROVE IT."

TRACE ADKINS

101

"THE ONLY THING [MY PARENTS] ASKED ME TO DO WAS TO PLEASE FINISH COLLEGE, AND I DID. THE GRADUATION CEREMONY WAS AT ELEVEN O'CLOCK IN THE MORNING, AND BY TWO O'CLOCK THAT AFTERNOON I WAS ON THE ROAD TO NASHVILLE, BECAUSE THAT'S WHERE MY TOTAL FOCUS WAS."

BILL ANDERSON

Country Music Hall of Famer Bill Anderson grew up in a time when the wishes of parents were expected to be taken seriously, but that didn't mean you couldn't still follow your dreams.

RESPECT YOUR ELDERS

102

"IT WAS THE MOST STABILITY I EVER HAD. [BUT] IT WAS REALLY HARD FOR THEM.... MY GRANDPA NEVER REALLY OFFICIALLY GOT TO RETIRE. HE HAD TO WORK JOBS ON THE SIDE. BUT I NEVER HAD TO DO WITHOUT."

KELLIE PICKLER

Kellie Pickler knows she was lucky to be raised in large part by her loving grandparents.

CHARLIE DANIELS

"DON'T GET ME WRONG, I LOVE TO HUNT AND FISH. I GREW UP DOING SO. BUT I'VE ALSO GROWN UP WITH A RESPECT FOR NATURE THAT I BELIEVE IS TAUGHT BY PEOPLE LIKE MY GRANDDADDY. THANKS TO HIM, I KNOW THE DIFFERENCE BETWEEN JUST KILLING SOMETHING FOR THE SAKE OF SHOOTING IT, AND HUNTING AND FISHING WITH RESPECT FOR MOTHER NATURE AND THE LAWS AND REGULATIONS WE HAVE IN PLACE TO PROTECT HER."

Messages about responsible outdoor sport carried a great deal of weight with Charlie Daniels because they came from an elder like a grandparent.

RESPECT YOUR ELDERS

104

CAM

"MY GRANDPA WOULD THROW WATER ON OUR FACES IN THE MORNING AND BE LIKE, 'IT'S SIX A.M., YOU GOTTA FEED THE HORSES IF YOU WANNA RIDE 'EM.'"

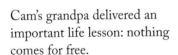

Cam's grandpa delivered an important life lesson: nothing comes for free.

After becoming a mother herself, Faith Hill has come to understand her birth mother's decision and what love for a child really means.

"I HAVE A LOT OF RESPECT FOR MY BIRTH MOTHER. I KNOW SHE MUST HAVE HAD A LOT OF LOVE FOR ME TO WANT TO GIVE WHAT SHE FELT WAS A BETTER CHANCE."

FAITH HILL

RESPECT YOUR ELDERS

Dan & Shay wrote a song called "From the Ground Up" about their grandparents' marriages.

"THEY WERE TOGETHER FOR SIXTY-FIVE YEARS, WHICH, THESE DAYS, WITH ALL THE DIVORCE AND STUFF IN THE MEDIA AND PRESS, IS A RARE THING. SO THAT'S SOMETHING THAT WE'D LIKE TO STRIVE FOR, AND SOMETHING WE'D LIKED TO HAVE IN OUR OWN LIVES."

DAN SMYERS
OF DAN & SHAY

"I HAVE THREE DAUGHTERS, SO I CAN'T BE AS TOUGH AS I WANT TO BE. WHEN YOU HAVE KIDS—ESPECIALLY DAUGHTERS—THEY KNOW HOW TO WORK YOU. THEY'RE A LOT SMARTER THAN WE ARE, THAT'S FOR SURE. BUT I'LL BE MORE TOUGH ON THEIR BOYFRIENDS."

TIM MCGRAW

Tim McGraw and Faith Hill's daughters might have famous parents, but the family dynamic is the same no matter who you are.

"MY SONS, I WANT TO CREATE A SENSE OF BEAUTY IN THEM THAT MOST ELEVEN-YEAR-OLDS DON'T HAVE. IF I CAN DO THAT, THAT SENSE OF BEAUTY WILL BE WITH THEM THE REST OF THEIR LIFE."

Kenny Rogers fathered twin boys late in life—when he was sixty-five years old.

KRIS KRISTOFFERSON

"SHE SAID THAT I WAS AN EMBARRASSMENT TO THE FAMILY. I'VE GIVEN THEM MOMENTS OF PRIDE—WHEN I GOT MY RHODES SCHOLARSHIP—BUT SHE SAID, 'THEY'LL NEVER MEASURE UP TO THE TREMENDOUS DISAPPOINTMENT YOU'VE ALWAYS BEEN.' WHY TELL YOUR KID THAT?"

Sadly, Kris Kristofferson learned a hard lesson about what not to do once we have children of our own.

LORETTA LYNN

"DADDY WAS REAL GENTLE WITH KIDS. THAT'S WHY I EXPECTED SO MUCH OUT OF MARRIAGE, FIGURING THAT ALL MEN SHOULD BE STEADY AND PLEASANT."

Loretta Lynn describes how her father's parenting style showed her how kindness can go a long way.

According to Willie Nelson, there's a very good reason corporal punishment was abandoned in his house!

"MY GRANDMOTHER SLAPPED A FART OUT OF ME ONE TIME THAT WHISTLED LIKE A FREIGHT TRAIN! IT SCARED BOTH OF US REALLY BAD. SHE NEVER HIT ME AGAIN."

WILLIE NELSON

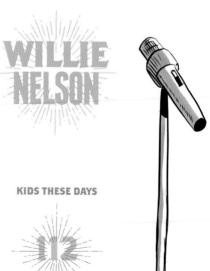

KIDS THESE DAYS

112

Kellie Pickler believes the key to a parent's balance between authority figure and ally is just having an open dialogue.

"I THINK THAT'S THE MOST IMPORTANT THING—TO KNOW THAT YOU CAN TALK ABOUT ANYTHING. I KNEW I COULD GO TO MY GRANDMA WITH ANYTHING IN THE WORLD. WHETHER I'D DONE SOMETHING BAD OR GOOD OR WHATEVER, I COULD GO AND TELL HER. I THINK IT'S ABOUT HAVING THAT FRIENDSHIP."

KELLIE PICKLER

"WE FEEL LIKE THE MOST MISUNDERSTOOD AND UNDERAP-PRECIATED MEMBERS OF OUR SOCIETY ARE THE FARMERS AND RANCHERS. WE HAVE THE GREATEST FARMERS IN THE WORLD, AND IT SEEMS LIKE WE DO EVERYTHING WE CAN TO DIS-COURAGE THEIR CREATIVITY AND PRODUCTIVITY, AND THAT'S BULL****. WE NEED TO MAKE IT COOL TO BECOME A FARMER OR A RANCHER."

RANDY OWEN
OF ALABAMA

Randy Owen and most country musicians agree on the need to preserve our agricultural roots.

"THE ISSUES THAT MATTER TO ME ARE THE SOCIAL SAFETY NETS FOR PEOPLE, HEALTH CARE, MIDDLE-CLASS CONCERNS. WE NEED TO TAKE CARE OF THE MIDDLE CLASS AND THE POOR IN OUR COUNTRY."

TIM MCGRAW

Some stars—including Tim McGraw— believe lifting up those who need help the most is the path to long-term prosperity.

JOE DON ROONEY
OF RASCAL FLATTS

"I FEEL LIKE WE'RE LOSING THE FABRIC OF WHAT MADE AMERICA AMERICA A LITTLE BIT. IT'S SLIPPING THROUGH OUR HANDS A LITTLE WHEN IT COMES TO THE CHRISTIANITY ON WHICH OUR FOREFATHERS FOUNDED THIS COUNTRY—PUTTING GOD FIRST."

Joe Don Rooney of Rascal Flatts sees the erosion of traditional Christian values as a significant concern.

THE WAY I SEE IT

DEAN SAMS OF LONESTAR

"YOU TAKE WHAT'S GOING ON IN THE WORLD RIGHT NOW—AND GOING ON IN AMERICA—AND WE NEED TO COME TOGETHER. WE NEED TO FIGURE OUT WAYS TO QUIT BICKERING AND BE THE STRONG UNITED STATES OF AMERICA THAT WE'VE ALWAYS BEEN."

When trouble seems to be on the horizon, Dean Sams of Lonestar hopes Americans can put aside their differences and stand united.

Patriotism can take many forms, and Willie Nelson thinks focusing on the wrong issues is a threat to America.

"I BELIEVE THIS COUNTRY WOULD BE BETTER OFF BRINGING ALL THE TROOPS HOME AND PUTTING THEM ON OUR OWN BORDERS TO STOP THE TRAFFICKING OF GUNS, DRUGS, AND PEOPLE. THIS IS OUR MAJOR PROBLEM. ALL THE MONEY THAT'S INVOLVED IN THIS KIND OF TRAFFICKING AND THE PRIVATIZATION OF PRISONS IS THE PROBLEM."

WILLIE NELSON

It's probably best to stick to music and steer clear of political discussion when interviewing Miranda Lambert.

"DEAR MR. WRITER AT THE *OTTAWA CITIZEN*: NEXT TIME [YOU] INTERVIEW ME, LET'S KEEP IT ABOUT THE MUSIC AND NOT ABOUT YOUR VIEW ON MY STANCE ON GUNS ... I DON'T TALK POLITICS, PERIOD. I'M NOT SURE ALL CANADIANS WOULD LIKE TO BE PUT IN YOUR CATEGORY. SPEAK FOR YOURSELF NOT YOUR COUNTRY. THX!"

MIRANDA LAMBERT
VIA TWITTER

COUNTRY STARS WITH FAMOUS *Parents*

PAM TILLIS
A star throughout the 1990s, Pam Tillis is the daughter of country singer, actor, and comedian Mel Tillis. She made her Grand Ole Opry debut at the age of eight.

SHOOTER JENNINGS
Shooter Jennings is the only son of outlaw icons Waylon Jennings and Jessie Colter. Like his parents, he blazes his own trail in country music.

HANK WILLIAMS JR.
Hank Jr. (born Randall Hank Williams) is the only son of country music's most revered artist—the late, great Hank Williams.

HOLLY WILLIAMS
Holly Williams, along with half-brother Shelton (known as Hank III), represents the third generation of the Hank Williams legacy.

AUBRIE SELLERS
Making her debut in 2016 with a gritty sound she calls "garage country," Aubrie Sellers is the daughter of sweet-singing Lee Ann Womack and songwriter Jason Sellers.

ROSANNE CASH
The eldest daughter of country legend Johnny Cash, Rosanne scored her first No. 1 in 1981 with the hit "Seven Year Ache."

THOMAS RHETT
If you knew Thomas Rhett by his real name—Thomas Rhett Akins Jr.—you'd see his sterling pedigree. His father is multi-platinum songwriter Rhett Akins.

JUSTIN TOWNES EARLE
Justin Townes Earle has followed a rebellious musical path just like his outspoken dad, Steve Earle.

JUNE CARTER CASH
If the Carter Family was the royal house of country music, June Carter Cash was its heiress. She began performing with the famous group at age ten in 1939.

HILLARY SCOTT
The only female member of the hit trio Lady Antebellum, Hillary Scott always looks poised in the spotlight—and that may be because her mother is '80s star Linda Davis.

chapter five

WORKING
man's blues

If there's one thing everyone living a country life knows, it's work—how to do it, how to be proud of it, how to be successful at it, and even how to get around doing too much of it. It's as inescapable as death and taxes, and has been a central hub of inspiration in the country music genre since the very beginning.

"THINK IT. BE IT. YOU ARE THE SUM TOTAL OF ALL YOUR THOUGHTS. REMEMBER YOU ARE WHO YOU WANTED TO BE. IF YOU'RE HAPPY, THANK GOD AND MOVE ON. IF YOU WANT TO CHANGE, YOU CAN."

WILLIE NELSON

At eighty-four years old, Willie Nelson has learned that a person is what he or she thinks about.

CHASE THOSE DREAMS

124

"HE TAUGHT ME THAT NOBODY WAS GONNA BE COMING TO YOUR FRONT DOOR TO FIND YOU AND SAY, 'I WANNA SIGN YOU TO A RECORD DEAL.' ANYTHING YOU WANT, YOU GOTTA GO OUT AND MAKE IT HAPPEN FOR YOURSELF. THAT STUCK WITH ME."

JASON ALDEAN

Jason Aldean's father gave him this advice while the Georgia native was struggling to find his way in Nashville.

KRISTIAN BUSH
OF SUGARLAND

"IF YOU SAY 'YES' ENOUGH, YOU WILL END UP GOING TO A PLACE YOU NEVER THOUGHT YOU WOULD GO."

According to Kristian Bush—solo artist and member of the duo Sugarland—what seems like a detour might actually be a stepping-stone.

CHASE THOSE DREAMS

DUSTIN LYNCH

"I CAN'T QUITE EXPLAIN WHY OR HOW I DID IT,
BUT I KNOW THIS, I'VE JUST HAD SOMETHING
INSIDE OF ME TELLING ME I COULD DO IT."

Dustin Lynch had little performing
experience when he moved to Nashville but talked his way onstage at the
famous Bluebird Cafe anyway.

For Justin Moore, there's always another mountain to climb … and another after that.

"WHEN I MOVED TO TOWN, ALL I WANTED TO DO WAS GET A RECORD DEAL. THEN WHEN I GOT A RECORD DEAL, ALL I WANTED TO DO WAS HAVE ONE HIT, AND THEN I WANTED TO HAVE ANOTHER AND PUT AN ALBUM OUT."

JUSTIN MOORE

The most successful country stars are those who never stop striving—even when they'd really like to—like Kenny Chesney.

"BEING A CREATIVE PERSON IS A CONSTANT ANNOYANCE, BECAUSE YOU'RE NEVER HAPPY AND YOU'RE ALWAYS THINK-ING. JUST WHEN YOU THINK YOU HAVE NOTHING TO DO, YOU THINK 'I'M NOT GOING TO WRITE A SONG TODAY,' THERE'S THIS THING … AND I SHOULDN'T SAY ANNOYANCE, BUT IT IS. SOMETIMES YOU WANT TO GO 'SHUT UP, LEAVE ME ALONE.'"

KENNY CHESNEY

"PERSEVERANCE IS ALWAYS THERE IN MY HEART AND SOUL. THAT WAS INSTILLED IN ME WITH MAMA AND DADDY, BECAUSE YOU DIDN'T QUIT, YOU DIDN'T GIVE UP. THAT'S WHAT I'VE ALWAYS TRIED TO PASS DOWN TO [MY SON] SHELBY. HE DOESN'T GIVE UP EITHER, AND I'M SO PROUD OF HIM."

REBA MCENTIRE

Reba McEntire's journey to stardom took years of struggle, and then on March 16, 1991, eight members of her band perished in a tragic plane crash.

"I STARTED TRYING TO DO WHAT I'M DOING RIGHT NOW, WHICH IS HAVE A LITTLE BIT OF MOMENTUM, HAVE SOME SONGS ON THE RADIO, ELEVEN YEARS AGO."

FRANKIE BALLARD

Nashville is known as a "ten-year over-night town," because stars like Frankie Ballard don't explode out of nowhere. They've actually been toiling away for years.

"IT JUST NEVER WENT ANYWHERE. WHEN YOU'RE DOING YOUR BEST AND IT'S NOT WORK-ING, YOU DON'T KNOW WHAT TO DO NEXT. THERE WERE ALWAYS THOSE ANGELS WHO KEPT ME BELIEVING IN MYSELF."

Keith Urban's early career seemed filled
with obstacles, but a strong support group
helped him keep going.

JOHNNY CASH

"WE HAD TO DO THIRTY-FIVE TAKES BEFORE WE GOT 'CRY! CRY! CRY!' RIGHT."

After thirty-five redos, Johnny Cash perfected the song that would launch his career.

The Randy Rogers Band scored a major label record deal, but then went back to a do-it-yourself arrangement.

"IF YOU CAN CONVINCE YOURSELF THAT YOU ACTUALLY BELIEVE AND GIVE YOURSELF THAT CONFIDENCE, THAT'S A GOOD FEELING. THAT'S THE MENTALITY I HAD. I HAD SOMETHING TO PROVE AGAIN. I WAS THE UNDERDOG AGAIN."

RANDY
ROGERS

David Lee Murphy scored a big hit with 1995's "Dust on the Bottle." But after his recording career slowed, he kept himself in the game as a songwriter.

"I THINK PERSEVERANCE IS THE KEY TO LONGEVITY. WE'RE LIKE THESE OLD, WHITE-BEARDED GUYS SITTING OUT IN A CREEK IN CALIFORNIA PANNING FOR GOLD EVERY DAY.... WE'RE SITTING OVER THERE STOOPED OVER THIS CREEK WITH A PAN, AND WE RUN ACROSS [A NUGGET] AND IT'S LIKE, 'DAMN, GOT ONE!'"

DAVID LEE
MURPHY

"COACH ALWAYS TOLD US, 'PRACTICE ALWAYS HAS TO BE HARDER THAN THE GAME.' JUST WORK REALLY, REALLY, REALLY HARD, SO WHEN YOU HIT SHOWTIME, THE SHOW IS ALMOST EASY."

TIM MCGRAW

Tim McGraw's father was Major League Baseball pitcher Tug McGraw, so he's always known about the work that's done behind the scenes.

"THERE'S A MILLION PEOPLE IN THIS WORLD THAT ARE MORE TALENTED THAN YOU AND I, BUT IT'S THE ONE THAT WORKS THE HARDEST THAT'S GOING TO GET THE JOB."

CHASE BRYANT

Superstar Tim McGraw gave Chase Bryant this advice, hoping to remind the young singer to focus and be diligent in his craft.

MERLE HAGGARD

"I ENJOY IT AS MUCH OR MORE THAN I EVER DID. IT'S KIND OF LIKE PITCHING A BASEBALL GAME. YOU'VE GOT TO STAY IN THAT RHYTHM."

For Merle Haggard, who racked up more than fifty years in the business, maintaining a steady pace of work was the key to going the distance.

KENNY CHESNEY

"THERE'S THIS PERCEPTION THAT I ONLY SING ABOUT PARTYING AND GETTING DRUNK. IF PEOPLE SAW HOW HARD I WORK, AND HOW MUCH THOUGHT WENT INTO EVERY MOVE WE MAKE, THEY WOULD BE ASTOUNDED."

Kenny Chesney is one of the hardest-working men in the industry—although most fans don't realize it.

If work starts to feel stale, Carrie Underwood might suggest finding some variety.

"I'M THE KIND OF PERSON WHO NEEDS TO SWITCH THINGS UP
AND TRY NEW THINGS AND SHAKE IT UP. THINGS END UP BET-
TER WHEN THEY'RE ON THE FLY AND A LITTLE UNEXPECTED.
EVERYBODY IS ON THE EDGE OF THEIR SEAT AND THEY'RE
READY FOR ANYTHING."

CARRIE
UNDERWOOD

This quote from Country Music Hall of Famer Bill Anderson is about as back-woods as it gets, but what he really meant is to always give your all.

"SOMEBODY TOLD ME YEARS AGO, 'IF YOU'RE GOING TO WRITE ABOUT FRYING ONIONS, MAKE THE READER OR THE LISTENER SMELL THOSE ONIONS,' AND I THINK THAT'S GOOD ADVICE."

BILL ANDERSON

"HERE I WAS PICKING COTTON IN THE HEAT AND THINKING, THERE'S A BETTER WAY TO MAKE A DOLLAR, AND A LIVING, THAN PICKING COTTON. [IT] WAS VERY HARD WORK BUT IN A LOT OF WAYS GOOD FOR ME BECAUSE IT MADE ME WORK HARDER ON MY GUITAR."

If Willie Nelson hadn't spent so much time picking cotton, he may never have had the inspiration to learn a new skill.

SWEAT EQUITY

"BECAUSE I GREW UP ON A FARM AND LEFT THE FARM AND WENT INTO THE MILITARY AND THEN WAS A MORNING DISC JOCKEY, I ALWAYS TOOK THE MORNINGS BECAUSE NOBODY WANTED TO GET UP THAT EARLY. I STILL DO IT, AND IT DROVE NASHVILLE CRAZY BECAUSE JUST WHEN EVERYBODY ELSE WAS GOING TO BED, I WAS GETTING UP AND WRITING."

Tom T. Hall has learned that procrastination is a cycle that gets harder and harder to escape.

LORETTA
LYNN

"IN THE LONG RUN, YOU MAKE YOUR OWN LUCK—GOOD, BAD, OR INDIFFERENT."

According to Loretta Lynn (and Roman philosopher Seneca), luck is what happens when preparation meets opportunity.

LUKE BRYAN

"I DON'T TURN DOWN MANY OPPORTUNITIES BECAUSE I'M ALL UP IN THE MIDDLE OF THIS. THIS IS WHAT I ASKED FOR. THIS IS WHAT I DREAMED OF. I WANTED ALL OF THIS, SO LET'S KEEP ON GOING AND GETTING IT."

Luke Bryan has learned that even after achieving your dream, you've got to keep chasing it.

Randy Houser discovered a need to reconnect with his passion for music.

"SOMETIMES YOU WALK INTO THE HOUSE AND YOU'VE HAD A BAD DAY AND YOU SEE YOUR GUITAR THERE AND PICK IT UP AND A PIECE OF A SONG WILL COME OUT, AND YOU GET EXCITED AND IT CHANGES EVERYTHING. IT'S ABOUT THE LOVE OF THAT MORE THAN IT IS ABOUT BEING FAMOUS OR ANY OF THAT OTHER STUFF. THAT STUFF COMES AND GOES, AND I'VE LEARNED THAT."

RANDY HOUSER

PAYDAY

John Rich—one half of the Big & Rich duo—made this observation about writing songs, but it can be applied to any endeavor.

"TO BE SUCCESSFUL IN SONGWRITING, YOU HAVE TO WRITE BECAUSE YOU LOVE IT, NOT BECAUSE YOU'RE DRIVEN TO GET RICH DOING IT."

JOHN RICH

"I STILL HAVE TO TAKE THE TRASH OUT. I TRIED TO BE LIKE, 'I HAVE A NO. 1 SONG,' BUT NOPE, I STILL HAVE TO TAKE THE TRASH OUT."

GEOFF SPRUNG
SONGWRITER AND
BASS PLAYER FOR
OLD DOMINION

Old Dominion's Geoff Sprung was just joking about being too big for trash duty. He hasn't lost sight of his "regular" self.

"YOU AREN'T WEALTHY UNTIL YOU HAVE SOMETHING MONEY CAN'T BUY."

GARTH BROOKS

In 2016, *Forbes* estimated Garth Brooks's income at seventy million dollars. And still, his three children are what he values the most.

TYLER FARR

"I WAS GOING NINETY-TO-NOTHING AND MY WORLD DID A 360. YOU'RE JUST TRYING TO CATCH 'EM WHILE THEY'RE BITING, AND YOU'RE DOING EVERYTHING YOU POSSIBLY CAN BECAUSE YOU GOT TO THAT POINT AND YOU WANT TO KEEP IT ROLLING."

When his career took off, Tyler Farr tried to do too much and developed a vocal cord condition that required surgery.

LUKE BRYAN

"IT'S LIKE WE'VE BEEN LIVING FOR ALBUM RELEASE FOR TWO MONTHS, AND NOW IT'S HERE, AND YOU'RE LIKE, WHAT DID WE DO THE TWO MONTHS TO GET UP HERE, OR EVEN SIX MONTHS? YOU GET SO FOCUSED ON A DAY, AND YOU DON'T REALIZE YOU'RE BURNING TIME IN BETWEEN THAT."

Luke Bryan became a platinum-selling superstar through a singular focus on his goal. But he learned the importance of building time into his schedule for real life.

In 2014, Kenny Chesney took an entire
year off from the road.

"IT WAS THE BEST DECISION I'VE EVER MADE—FOR MYSELF AS
AN INDIVIDUAL, MY RELATIONSHIPS, MY FRIENDSHIPS. I'M A
LOT EASIER TO BE AROUND NOW. THERE WAS ALSO A LITTLE
BIT OF EXHAUSTION IN THERE, HONESTLY."

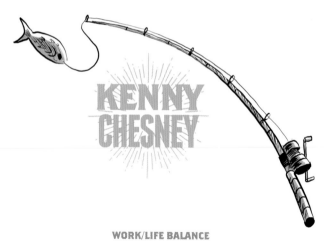

KENNY
CHESNEY

WORK/LIFE BALANCE

At twenty-six years old, Thomas Rhett had notched six No. 1 hits in a row, but the nonstop cycle left no time to appreciate his accomplishments.

"I WANT TO TAKE MORE TIME TO SIT BACK AND ENJOY THE GOOD THINGS THAT ARE HAPPENING WHILE THEY'RE HAPPENING, INSTEAD OF JUST CRUISING THROUGH THE GOOD MOMENTS TO GET TO THE NEXT ONE."

THOMAS RHETT

"BACK IN THE HEYDAY—WHEN WE WERE RUNNING CRAZY AND HAVING THREE NO. 1S A YEAR, APPEARING ON TELEVISION AND GOING AROUND THE WORLD—WE NEVER TOOK THE TIME TO ENJOY IT. IT'S A LITTLE LESS STRESSFUL NOWADAYS ... AND I THINK WE TAKE THE TIME TO REFLECT ON WHAT WE'RE DOING."

RICHIE MCDONALD
OF LONESTAR

Lonestar have "been there, done that." Their only regret is that they didn't stop to smell the roses often enough.

WORK/LIFE BALANCE

"THERE IS A FINE LINE BETWEEN BEING DRIVEN AND BEING SELFISH. AND I THINK I CROSSED THAT LINE WITH MY OTHER KIDS. I MEAN, WE'RE GOOD WITH EACH OTHER NOW AND ALL THAT. BUT I REALLY WANT TO TRY TO BE BETTER WITH MY TWO YOUNG BOYS."

KENNY ROGERS

In the 1970s and '80s, Kenny Rogers was one of country's biggest stars, meaning there was little time for family life. Luckily, Rogers got a second chance when he and wife Wanda had twin boys in 2004.

BEFORE THEY
were famous

THE MOST SURPRISING
COUNTRY STAR DAY JOBS

ERIC CHURCH
PHONE OPERATOR FOR A HOME-SHOPPING NETWORK

Eric Church took late-night orders over the phone for a home-shopping network in Nashville and was fired for trying to talk drunk people out of completing their purchases.

TOBY KEITH
SEMIPRO FOOTBALL PLAYER FOR THE OKLAHOMA CITY DRILLERS

When he wasn't fronting his band in local bars, Toby Keith was on the football field playing defensive end for the semi-pro Oklahoma City Drillers. He tried out for the Oklahoma Outlaws USFL team, but didn't make the cut.

KRIS KRISTOFFERSON
HELICOPTER PILOT

Kris Kristofferson is truly a man of many talents. Before becoming one of the most celebrated songwriters in history

and an award-winning actor, he was a Rhodes Scholar, an Army Ranger, and a helicopter pilot, flying men and supplies back and forth to oil rigs in the Gulf of Mexico.

TRISHA YEARWOOD
COUNTRY MUSIC HALL OF FAME TOUR GUIDE

When Trisha Yearwood needed a job during her studies at Nashville's Belmont University, she scored a dream gig—giving tours in the Country Music Hall of Fame and Museum. In 2015, she came full circle by earning her own exhibit in the museum.

MARTINA McBRIDE
MERCHANDISE SALES FOR GARTH BROOKS

While Martina McBride was selling T-shirts for Garth Brooks, her husband John (a sound engineer) got Garth to promise to let Martina open shows for him, provided she could land a record contract. She did so, and Garth kept his word, later jokingly referring to himself as "a genius" for making the deal.

CARRIE UNDERWOOD
GAS STATION ATTENDANT

Carrie Underwood had a number of jobs before making it big on *American Idol*, including as a veterinary assistant. But her first job was at a gas station convenience store near her home in Oklahoma while she was still in high school.

chapter six

FOR THE

good times

After the work is done, country folks sure do know how to enjoy themselves. It doesn't take much—maybe a fishing pole, a mud pit, or just a backyard bonfire—plus a little liquid inspiration and some country music, of course.

KELSEA BALLERINI

"ME AND MY WHOLE BAND WALKED INTO IT WITH A REALLY OPEN MIND AND OPEN HEART. THAT'S WHY WE'VE HAD SO MUCH FUN. I STILL THINK I'M NAÏVE, AND I LOVE IT BECAUSE I DON'T EVER WANT TO THINK I KNOW HOW IT ALL WORKS—EVER."

As one of country's youngest stars when she spoke these words, Kelsea Ballerini was holding on to that youthful sense of wonder.

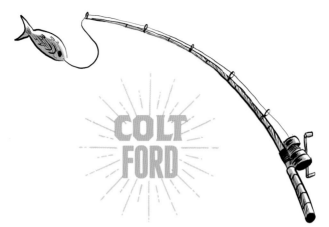

COLT
FORD

"DON'T SWEAT THE SMALL STUFF. BECAUSE IN THE END, IT'S ALL SMALL STUFF."

If Colt Ford spent all his time worrying about things that went wrong, he'd miss out on all that's going right.

As a songwriter, Tom T. Hall knows how big of an impact perception has on us all. Problems and worries are easier to tackle if we can visualize them.

"IT WAS SOMETHING I HEARD A PSYCHIATRIST SAY ONCE: 'PEOPLE SHOULD GET UP IN THE MORNINGS AND JUST WRITE DOWN ALL THEIR PET PEEVES.' IT'S THE MOST ASTOUNDING THING YOU CAN DO, BECAUSE YOU START THAT AND REALIZE HOW LITTLE YOU HAVE TO WORRY ABOUT. THE LIST IS NOT GOING TO BE NEARLY AS LONG AS YOU'D THINK IT WOULD BE, AND PEOPLE ARE ALWAYS AMAZED AT HOW LITTLE THEY REALLY HAVE TO BE PISSED ABOUT."

TOM T. HALL

Willie Nelson knows that whatever it is you love to do—riding horses, boating, relaxing in your favorite chair—you should do it often.

"THE WORLD LOOKS BETTER ON A HORSE."

WILLIE NELSON

"HAPPINESS IS A CHOICE. WE'VE BEEN SO SUCCESSFUL. SOMEONE WHO DOESN'T GET TO LIVE THE LIFE WE LIVE MIGHT PUT US UP AGAINST A BILLION-SELLING ARTIST LIKE GARTH BROOKS OR GEORGE STRAIT AND SAY WE DIDN'T GET TO THAT LEVEL.... FOR US, IT'S A LITTLE DIFFERENT."

RANDY ROGERS
OF THE RANDY ROGERS BAND

Texas country favorites the Randy Rogers Band might not be superstars, but they love what they do.

"I LOVE TO LAUGH. A DAY WITHOUT LAUGHING IS A SIN TO ME, AND I'M TALKING BELLY LAUGHS. THOSE KEEP ME GOING."

LORRIE MORGAN

According to '90s country star Lorrie Morgan, there's something revitalizing about laughter.

LUKE BRYAN

"I LIKE TO HUNT, FISH, RIDE AROUND ON MY FARM, BUILD A BIG BONFIRE, AND DRINK SOME BEERS—AND THAT'S WHAT I SING ABOUT."

Luke Bryan knows the importance of staying true to yourself.

WILLIE NELSON

"YOU WILL NEVER FIND HAPPINESS UNTIL YOU STOP LOOKING FOR IT."

At eighty-four years old, Willie Nelson has learned that fun will often come to you if you let it.

Brad Paisley doesn't care what it looks like. If you enjoy doing something—even if it looks crazy—have at it.

"I SHOOT A BOW A LOT. I'VE GOT A BUNCH OF TARGETS. I'VE GOT BEARS AND VELOCIRAPTORS AND COYOTE TARGETS ALL OVER THE FARM. IT LOOKS LIKE IT'S THE WORST ZOO YOU'VE EVER SEEN … IT LOOKS LIKE I'M A NUT. BUT I GO OUT ON THE PORCH IN THE MORNING WITH A CUP OF COFFEE AND JUST SHOOT."

Longtime friends can be like a rope tying you to who you really are, says Jason Aldean.

"A LOT OF THE FRIENDS I HANG OUT WITH NOW, A LOT OF THEM ARE STILL GUYS I GREW UP WITH IN HIGH SCHOOL."

JASON
ALDEAN

"EVEN ON THE WEEKENDS, YOU MIGHT SEE FIFTEEN PEOPLE OUT HERE. IF WE KEPT GOING A COUPLE OF MILES DOWN THE RIVER, THERE'S A SANDBAR THAT NEVER MOVES WITH A VOL-LEYBALL NET, AND THAT'S 'REDNECK ISLAND.'"

JAKE OWEN

Having a secret spot to kick back can do wonders for a person's state of mind, and Jake Owen's found that on a peaceful river just outside Nashville.

"FRIENDS WITH TRACTORS, MAN. THAT WILL GET YOU OUT OF ANYTHING. IF YOUR FRIEND HAS A TRACTOR, HE CAN TEAR YOUR HOUSE DOWN, HE CAN PULL YOUR TRUCK OUT OF THE MUD, HE CAN PLANT YOUR FIELD, HE CAN GROW YOUR GRO-CERIES—HE CAN DO WHATEVER YOU WANT TO DO."

DALLAS DAVIDSON

To the cowriter of backwoods hits like "Rain Is a Good Thing" and "Boys 'Round Here," it never hurts to have friends who are country boys.

"WHY WOULD YOU WANT TO GO STAND IN LINE AND WEAR BLACK TIES AND PAY TWENTY DOLLARS FOR A MARTINI WHEN YOU CAN GO OUT AND HAVE A GREAT TIME AND KICK SOME DUST UP IN A FIELD?"

For country folks like Luke Bryan, the best bar scene in the world is a cooler on a tailgate and an old patch of dirt.

COLE SWINDELL

"I THINK BEER ALWAYS LEADS TO A GOOD TIME.... BEER'S EVEN IN MY NEW SONG 'YOU SHOULD BE HERE.' THAT ONE'S ABOUT HOW I REMEMBER SITTING DOWN AND, NOT GETTING CRAZY, BUT SHARING A BEER WITH MY DAD. WE COULD HAVE HAD THE MEMORY WITHOUT IT, BUT HAVING A BEER WAS A PART OF LIFE."

Enjoying an adult beverage is not always about partying for Cole Swindell. Some-times it just provides a reason to stop and connect with someone you love.

Blake Shelton likes to tease his friend and co-judge of *The Voice*, Adam Levine, but he's right that drinking with friends is much better than drinking alone.

"I GET FRUSTRATED WITH ADAM [LEVINE] BECAUSE, TO ME, ROCK STARS ARE SUPPOSED TO BE DRUNK ALL THE TIME. BUT HE'S VERY HEALTHY. HE TAKES CARE OF HIMSELF. AND IT DRIVES ME CRAZY, BECAUSE I WANT HIM TO BE MORE LIKE ME."

BLAKE SHELTON

SOCIAL LUBRICATION

Miranda Lambert is often surrounded
by fans having the time of their lives, but
there's a time and a place for everything.

"I HAVE ONE BEFORE A SHOW AND A HALF DURING. LATER, IF I WANT TO THROW DOWN, I THROW DOWN!"

"I'M THE KIND OF GUY, WHEN WE'RE IN THE MIDDLE-OF-NO-WHERE IOWA AND WE'RE ALL SITTING AROUND THE BUS IN A TENT, PASSING AROUND WINE AND WHISKEY BOTTLES, I'LL GET WITH IT UNTIL FOUR OR FIVE IN THE MORNING IN THOSE KINDS OF SETTINGS. I'LL DANCE A JIG AND DRINK ALL NIGHT, BUT WHEN I GO TO VEGAS—WHERE YOU'RE SUPPOSED TO BE THAT WAY—I GET REALLY WITHDRAWN. IT'S A WEIRD THING."

KIP MOORE

Choosing to drink comes with respon-sibility—to those around you and to yourself. Kip Moore knows where he feels comfortable and where he doesn't.

SOCIAL LUBRICATION

"THE ONLY TIME I FEEL AWKWARD IS WHEN PEOPLE THAT DO DRINK DON'T DRINK AROUND ME. THE BENEFITS [TO BEING SOBER] ARE WHEN A SINGLE GIRL NEEDS A RIDE HOME, I'M LIKE 'HEY I'LL BE YOUR HUCKLEBERRY!' AND IF YOU GET IN A FIGHT, YOU HAVE A LITTLE BIT OF AN ADVANTAGE."

BRANTLEY GILBERT

Drinking isn't for everyone, but that doesn't mean you can't still have a good time. Just ask Brantley Gilbert.

Willie's Words

Truth be told, Willie Nelson's sense of humor is almost as legendary as his music. A mix of dry observation and off-color innuendo, his bag of jokes and one-liners often seems bottomless.

"I'VE BEEN CALLED A TROUBLEMAKER A TIME OR TWO," HE SAYS IN HIS MEMOIR, *ROLL ME UP AND SMOKE ME WHEN I DIE.* "WHAT THE HELL IS A TROUBLEMAKER? WELL, IT'S SOMEONE WHO MAKES TROUBLE. LIKE IT OR NOT, LOVE IT OR NOT, HE WILL STIR IT UP. WHY? BECAUSE IT NEEDS STIRRING UP!"

"DID YOU HEAR ABOUT THE NERVOUS BANK ROBBER? HE SAID 'STICK UP YOUR *** OR I'LL BLOW YOUR HANDS OFF!'"

WILLIE'S JOKES

"A GUY WAS COMING OUT OF AN ANTIQUE SHOP WITH A BIG GRANDFATHER CLOCK, BUMPED INTO A DRUNK AND FELL DOWN, SMASHING THE CLOCK. HE SAID TO THE DRUNK 'WHY DON'T YOU WATCH WHERE YOU'RE GOING?' THE DRUNK SAID 'WHY DON'T YOU WEAR A WRISTWATCH LIKE EVERYBODY ELSE?'"

"A DRUNK FELL OUT OF A SECOND-FLOOR WINDOW. A GUY CAME RUNNING OVER AND ASKED, 'WHAT HAPPENED?' THE DRUNK SAID, 'I DON'T KNOW, I JUST GOT HERE.'"

"THESE GUYS WERE PLAYING GOLF ONE DAY WHEN A FUNERAL PASSED BY ON THE ROAD NEXT TO THE GOLF COURSE. ONE OF THE PLAYERS TOOK OFF HIS HAT AND WAITED UNTIL THE PROCESSION PASSED. ONE OF HIS FELLOW GOLFERS SAID, 'JOHN, THAT'S MIGHTY RESPECTABLE OF YOU TO DO THAT.' THE GUY SAID, 'IT'S THE LEAST I CAN DO FOR HER. WE WOULD HAVE BEEN MARRIED TWENTY YEARS TODAY.'"

BEST COUNTRY MUSIC vacations

TORTUGA MUSIC FESTIVAL
Held each spring on the sun-kissed beach of Fort Lauderdale, Florida, the Tortuga Music Festival is a giant, three-day beach party that draws thousands of fans and some of the biggest names in country music.

LUKE BRYAN'S CRASH MY PLAYA
Held each year since 2015, Luke Bryan's Crash My Playa is the perfect way to escape the winter months in tropical, country-music style. Each ticket gets fans four days of all-inclusive fun in Riviera Maya, Mexico, plus access to massive beachside concerts each night.

THE COUNTRY MUSIC CRUISE
Simply put, the Country Music Cruise is a luxury music festival at sea. The weeklong trip sails fans to various Caribbean paradises, all while big-name artists perform on the ship. And since everyone is "in the same boat," there's plenty of opportunity to bump into the stars.

CMA Music Festival

Each year in June about 100,000 country fans from around the world descend on Nashville, Tennessee, to celebrate the music they love in its hometown. Hundreds of artists are on hand for fan club parties, meet and greets, and autograph sessions, while massive, stadium-filling super concerts put the biggest names on one stage for four nights in a row.

chapter seven

LOVE MAKES
the world go 'round

The sheer volume of love songs in country music shows just how important matters of the heart are to country stars. The harder they fall, the better the story, and like most things in life, love's always adapting.

"IF YOU'RE IN LOVE, YOU'RE IN LOVE. IT DOESN'T MATTER. LOVE IS LOVE IS LOVE IS LOVE. YOUR HEART CAN'T HELP WHAT IT DOES."

DOLLY PARTON

To Dolly Parton, it's almost like the heart has a mind of its own.

DATING AND ROMANCE

"SHE ALWAYS MADE ME WANT TO BE BETTER FOR ME."

BRANTLEY GILBERT

Brantley Gilbert thought of himself as a guy who'd be "single for life," but that changed when he started dating a girl he grew up with who knew who he truly was.

"I WAS ENTHRALLED. HERE WAS THIS VIVACIOUS, EXUBERANT, FUNNY, HAPPY GIRL, AS TALENTED AND SPIRITED AND STRONG-WILLED AS THEY COME, AND SHE WAS BRINGING OUT THE BEST IN ME. IT FELT WONDERFUL."

When Johnny Cash began dating June Carter, he was completely consumed by thoughts of her. Sometimes you just know.

DATING AND ROMANCE

BLAKE SHELTON

"SHE BECAME MY CLOSEST ALLY, MY FRIEND, MY PERSON IN MY LIFE WHO HAD MY BACK, AND I HAD HERS. [I] CREATED THIS BOND WITH SOMEBODY THAT I NEVER WOULD HAVE THOUGHT [OF] IN A MILLION YEARS."

Following his second divorce, Blake Shelton found solace in a new relationship with pop singer Gwen Stefani.

Having an open mind is only a tiny piece of the romance puzzle. One of the most important things is to know who you are and what you want, says Hunter Hayes.

"I DON'T KNOW IF I HAVE A TYPE, BUT I REALLY LIKE GIRLS WHO ARE DRIVEN. I REALLY CARE ABOUT MUSIC, SO I LIKE IT WHEN A GIRL REALLY CARES ABOUT SOMETHING, TOO. CONFIDENCE IS A BIG THING FOR ME. I STRUGGLED WITH FEELING CONFIDENT FOR A LONG TIME, BUT I THINK IT'S IMPORTANT TO BE STRONG AND NOT COMPROMISE FOR A RELATIONSHIP."

HUNTER HAYES

In 2007 Carrie Underwood still hadn't met her future husband, hockey player Mike Fisher. But since her heart was in the right place, it was only a matter of time.

"I'M NOT SAYING I WANT TO GET MARRIED TOMORROW, BUT I'D LIKE TO HAVE SOMEONE OTHER THAN MY MOM TO CALL WHEN I HAVE GOOD NEWS."

CARRIE UNDERWOOD

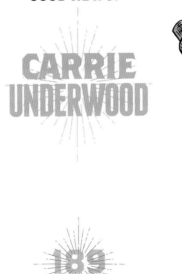

"I WAS REALLY CARRYING THE TORCH FOR THE SINGLE DUDE, AND MY WHOLE MANTRA WAS ABOUT BEING SINGLE. IT WAS LIKE A TRAIN GOING FULL SPEED, [TOURING] THREE HUNDRED DATES A YEAR. I MET MY WIFE, AND I WAS LIKE, 'OK, JUMP ON THE TRAIN.' BUT IT DOESN'T WORK THAT WAY. YOU HAVE TO GET ON A DIFFERENT TRAIN."

DIERKS BENTLEY

Dierks Bentley knows marriage is not the same as dating, and there are a new set of rules for making it work.

'TIL DEATH DO US PART

"YOU CAN CALL ME WHIPPED, WHATEVER YOU WANT. I JUST HAVE TO BE BREATHING THE SAME AIR SHE IS."

For country royalty like Garth Brooks and Trisha Yearwood, closeness is the key.

KELLIE PICKLER

"SPENDING TIME APART, WE HAVE TIME TO APPRECIATE THE THINGS WE LOVE ABOUT EACH OTHER. IF WE HAVE TO GO TWO WEEKS WITHOUT SEEING EACH OTHER, WHEN WE DO SEE EACH OTHER, YOU CAN'T KEEP US AWAY FROM ONE ANOTHER."

Absence has been known to make the heart grow fonder. When Kellie Pickler can't be with her husband, songwriter Kyle Jacobs, she keeps that in mind.

'TIL DEATH DO US PART

KEITH URBAN

"SHE RISKED EVERYTHING TO TRUST ME AND PULL ME OUT OF THE FIRE."

Shortly after Keith Urban married actress Nicole Kidman, his drug use caught up with him. Kidman stood by him and may have saved his life.

While Miranda Lambert and Blake Shelton's marriage didn't last, she came away with a better understanding of what it's all about.

"IF I EVER WERE TO GET MARRIED AGAIN—WHICH IS COMPLETELY NOT ON MY RADAR AT ALL RIGHT NOW—I FEEL LIKE IT'S NOT ABOUT IT BEING A STEP IN LIFE. IT'S NOT ABOUT A PIECE OF PAPER OR A DIAMOND. IT'S THE WAY YOU FEEL ABOUT SOMEBODY AND THE COMMITMENT IN YOUR HEART."

MIRANDA LAMBERT

'TIL DEATH DO US PART

194

For Carrie Underwood, marriage is more important than anything else in her life—even her career in country music.

"IF MIKE EVER TOLD ME HE NEEDED ME TO QUIT, I'D QUIT. WHEN YOU MAKE THAT PROMISE TO SOMEBODY, AND YOU STAND BEFORE GOD AND YOUR FAMILY AND FRIENDS, YOU'VE GOT TO DO EVERYTHING THAT YOU POSSIBLY CAN TO MAKE THAT WORK."

CARRIE UNDERWOOD

"YOU KNOW, FIFTY YEARS IS A LONG TIME, ESPECIALLY IN THIS BUSINESS. WE'VE WORKED OUT REALLY WELL. MY HUSBAND IS SUCH A LONER, AND I'M JUST ALL OVER THE PLACE AND I LOVE TO BE WITH PEOPLE.... HE'S BEEN THE PERFECT PARTNER FOR ME. AND I THINK I'M ALSO THE PERFECT PERSON FOR HIM, TOO, BECAUSE HE'S SUCH A WEIRDO. NO OTHER WOMAN WOULD HAVE PUT UP WITH HIM, BUT NO OTHER MAN WOULD PUT UP WITH ME. I GUESS GOD SAW FIT TO PUT US TOGETHER."

DOLLY PARTON

Dolly Parton's marriage to her husband has flourished because each one allows the other to be themselves.

"I'VE OBSERVED THE WAY PEOPLE RECKLESSLY TOSS AROUND THE WORD 'LOVE.' ... I FEEL LIKE WHAT THAT WORD EMBODIES, IT'S GOTTA BE SELFLESS. I THINK SO OFTEN WHEN WE USE THE WORD 'LOVE,' IT'S A BLANKET OF SECURITY. IT'S TO KEEP THE PLAYING FIELD EVEN, AND IT'S 'I LOVE YOU, AS LONG AS IT'S UNDER THESE CONDITIONS.'"

KIP MOORE

Kip Moore has seen true love, and he's seen the fake kind. For any relationship to last, he figures the commitment has to be unconditional.

LUKE BRYAN

"I THINK THE IMPORTANT THING IS THAT WE TRY TO COMMUNICATE AS MUCH AS WE CAN. IF WE HAVE A LITTLE HICCUP WITH ONE ANOTHER, WE TALK IT OUT, FIGURE IT OUT, CLOSE THE BOOK ON IT, AND MOVE ON DOWN THE ROAD."

Luke Bryan and his wife Caroline have grown from college sweethearts into parents with schedules that often keep them apart, but communication has helped them weather every storm.

EVERLASTING LOVE

ALAN JACKSON

"WE TRY TO GET OUT AND GO TO DINNER OR HANG OUT AND GO TO THE MOVIES OR SOMETHING. WE BUILD A FIRE AND HAVE SOME WINE AND A NICE EVENING."

For Alan Jackson and his wife Denise, lasting love is no accident. They do their best to continue dating each other.

Josh Turner sees love as a spiritual thing that needs to be taken seriously if it's to last.

"I HEARD BILLY GRAHAM TALKING ABOUT HOW A LOT OF PEOPLE TREAT LOVE CASUALLY, THEY DON'T TREAT IT WITH RESPECT, AND THEY DON'T HAVE REVERENCE FOR IT. IT JUST REALLY STRUCK A CHORD WITH ME. YOU SEE A LOT OF PEOPLE PUSHING MARRIAGE TO THE WAYSIDE AND NOT REALLY TAKING IT THROUGH."

JOSH TURNER

In order to keep the spark alive, sometimes we have to take matters into our own hands. Part of Carrie Underwood's recipe involves staying in top physical condition.

"EVEN WHEN HE'S LIKE, 'I'M SO OUT OF SHAPE,' HE STILL HAS A SIX-PACK. HAVING MIKE THERE, I WANT TO BE A HOT WIFE!"

LONGEST-RUNNING COUNTRY love stories

TIM MCGRAW AND FAITH HILL

Tim and Faith met while on tour in 1996, and although Hill was engaged at the time, she knew she had found her soul mate. The pair was married that same year.

CLINT BLACK AND LISA HARTMAN BLACK

One was a country star at the top of his game and the other a famous actress. After a "secret" courtship, they married in 1991.

MARTINA AND JOHN MCBRIDE

Martina McBride married her husband John in 1988, well before she was famous. He actually helped her career take off by introducing her to his boss at the time, Garth Brooks.

JOHNNY CASH AND JUNE CARTER CASH

Married from 1968 until both passed away in 2003, the love story of Johnny and June has been immortalized in song and on film—but there are still longer love stories.

ALAN AND DENISE JACKSON

Alan Jackson married his high school sweetheart Denise in 1979, and after raising three daughters, he says they're now happier together than ever.

DOLLY PARTON AND CARL DEAN

Dolly and Carl are an odd couple of sorts but balance each other perfectly: he likes to stay out of the spotlight, and she relishes it. Though rarely seen in public, their love has been strong for more than fifty years. They were married in 1966.

chapter eight

WHEN IT ALL

falls apart

Country stars know all about hard times, whether they're based on problems of the heart, problems of the pocketbook, or a dream that refuses to come true. Resiliency is built into their DNA and a big part of the country character.

"I THINK WE ARE SHAPED BY OUR DECISIONS, AND OFTENTIMES BY OUR BAD DECISIONS MORE THAN OUR GOOD ONES."

BRANDY CLARK

Nobody's perfect, and sometimes—as Brandy Clark knows—we learn more from our mistakes than our success.

"IF EVERYTHING FAILS, START OVER. FAILURE IS NOT FATAL. IT'S INEVITABLE THAT YOU LEARN FROM YOUR MISTAKES."

WILLIE NELSON

Willie Nelson has learned that messing up isn't the end of the world.

MAREN MORRIS

"I THINK ABOUT ALL OF THE TALENT SHOWS I'VE TRIED OUT FOR IN MY LIFE, AND I'M SO GLAD I DIDN'T MAKE ANY OF THEM. I WAS REJECTED FROM *THE VOICE*. I WAS REJECTED FROM *AMERICAN IDOL*—AND I'M HAPPIER FOR IT NOW."

For Maren Morris, TV talent-show rejection let her start with a blank slate when fame came calling.

SCOTTY McCREERY

"YOU'VE GOT TO GO THROUGH THE VALLEYS BEFORE YOU CAN REACH THE TOP OF THE MOUNTAIN."

Former *American Idol* winner Scotty McCreery had a wide valley ahead of him after abruptly parting ways with his record label.

After emerging from the tragedy of losing loved ones, Luke Bryan and his family feel compelled to reassure others that brighter days will eventually return.

"WHAT'S HAPPENED IN MY PERSONAL LIFE, WITH ALL THE LOSS IN MY FAMILY—OUR MODUS OPERANDI OF ALL THAT IS TO HELP PEOPLE. IF THEY CAN UNDERSTAND THEY'RE NOT ALONE IN CHALLENGES, AND IF I CAN SMILE THROUGH IT, MAYBE THEY CAN."

LUKE BRYAN

WHAT DOESN'T KILL YOU ...

A divorce and remarriage turned Jason Aldean's life upside down, but he ended up wiser and ultimately happier for the experience.

"I HAVE MADE MISTAKES, BUT I AM A BETTER PERSON BECAUSE OF IT AND WOULDN'T CHANGE A THING."

JASON ALDEAN

"IT SEEMS PEOPLE ARE SEARCHING FOR SOME-THING AND THEY FIND IT IN SOMEBODY, BUT THEN IT GOES AWAY LATER ON. LOVE IS SUCH A MYSTERIOUS THING."

Like many people, Dierks Bentley wonders what makes the heart so unpredictable.

"I OFTEN THINK WHAT ATTRACTS US TO PEOPLE EVEN-TUALLY REPELS US."

BRANDY CLARK

Without balance, Brandy Clark knows,
even the things we love about our partners
might eventually lead to a breakup.

WILLIE
NELSON

"THEY SAY THERE ARE NO EX-WIVES, ONLY ADDITIONAL WIVES, AND THAT'S NOT SUCH A BAD THING, ESPECIALLY IF YOU HAD KIDS TOGETHER. IT'S GOOD TO STAY ON GOOD TERMS WITH EVERYONE."

Willie Nelson has been married four times, but he figures once you've married someone, they'll always be a part of your life.

BREAK UP WHEN IT'S BROKEN

CHRIS YOUNG

"I DON'T THINK BREAKUPS ARE EVER EASY FOR ANYBODY. IF THEY ARE, THEY AREN'T MUCH OF A BREAKUP."

To Chris Young, no two breakups are the same. And the more it hurts, the more we learn.

Kip Moore might not be able to take back what happened in a breakup, but he can at least do better next time.

"THE DEFINITION OF INSANITY IS DOING THE SAME THING OVER AND OVER AGAIN AND EXPECTING A DIFFERENT RESULT, AND THAT'S KIND OF LIKE MY APPROACH WITH WOMEN.... IF SOMETHING GOES WRONG AND I'VE REALLY HURT SOMEBODY'S FEELINGS THROUGH A BREAKUP, I DON'T JUST MOVE TO THE NEXT THING AND NOT TRY TO LEARN FROM WHAT TOOK PLACE."

BREAK UP WHEN IT'S BROKEN

Sometimes, as Loretta Lynn suggests, a relationship not worth fighting for means you're better off alone.

"IF YOU CAN'T FIGHT FOR YOUR MAN, HE'S NOT WORTH HAVING."

LORETTA LYNN

"I JUST WANT TO LIVE A LIFE FULL OF EVERYTHING. SOME OF THAT MIGHT MEAN NIGHTS ON MY PORCH CRYING, DRINKING WHISKEY, AND GOING, 'MAN, THIS SUCKS RIGHT NOW.' BUT IT'S ABOUT LIVING IN THE MOMENT AND FEELING EVERY TINGE OF PAIN, THEN WAKING UP THE NEXT DAY AND GOING, 'ALL RIGHT, I'M GOING TO RIDE MY PONIES. I'M GOING TO HAVE A GIRLS' NIGHT.'"

MIRANDA LAMBERT

Following her divorce from Blake Shelton, Miranda Lambert knew there would be some tough times. But healing required her not to shy away from her emotions.

MOVING ON

"YOU NEVER GET OVER LOSING A CHILD, YOU ONLY GET THROUGH IT."

WILLIE NELSON

Some things are just too much to fully overcome, as Willie Nelson learned after his son Billy died in 1991.

HUNTER HAYES

"SOME TIME HAS TO PASS, BUT WHY NOT BE BUDS? YOU BOTH HAD A LEARNING EXPERIENCE AND IT WAS HARD, AND FOR SOME PEOPLE IT'S HARDER THAN OTHERS. BUT WHAT YOU WENT THROUGH SHAPES WHO YOU ARE NOW AND WHO YOU'RE GOING TO BE. YOU CAN BE THANKFUL FOR THAT."

Call him an idealist, but Hunter Hayes can even find the silver lining in a breakup—and he believes that exes can still be friends.

KRISTIAN BUSH
OF SUGARLAND

"I'M HERE IN MY BOOTS LIVING. I DON'T LOOK BEHIND ME BECAUSE I'M NOT GOING IN THAT DIRECTION. I AM LOOKING AHEAD."

After a tragic stage collapse killed seven fans before a Sugarland concert in 2011, the duo was racked with grief. But they eventually had to force themselves back into daily life.

Even though country stars Lorrie Morgan and Sammy Kershaw were divorced in 2007, she's still working through it in song.

"SOMETIMES FOR ME IT'S GOOD TO GO BACK AND RELIVE MOMENTS LIKE THAT, BECAUSE EVEN THOUGH YOU GET OVER SOMETHING, YOU NEVER REALLY GET RID OF THE PAIN. EACH SONG BRINGS BACK SOMETHING THAT NEEDS TO MOVE IN ME."

LORRIE MORGAN

MOVING ON

When Reba McEntire's twenty-six-year marriage to Narvel Blackstock came to an end in 2016, it was a shock, but she decided it was ultimately for the best.

"THE DIVORCE WAS NOT MY IDEA. I DIDN'T WANT IT IN ANY SHAPE, FORM, OR FASHION. SO, IT WAS REALLY HARD TO MAKE THE ADJUSTMENT WHEN SOMEONE'S NOT HAPPY.... I JUST THOUGHT IT WAS THE BEST THING TO TAKE MY MARBLES AND GO PLAY SOME-WHERE ELSE, IS WHAT DADDY USED TO ALWAYS SAY."

REBA
MCENTIRE

COUNTRY'S WISEST
TITLES ABOUT heartbreak

"(IF YOU'RE NOT IN IT FOR LOVE) I'M OUTTA HERE!"
—SHANIA TWAIN

Shania Twain wasn't playing games with her heart back in 1995. You've got to respect a woman who knows what she wants.

"HERE'S A QUARTER (CALL SOMEONE WHO CARES)"
—TRAVIS TRITT

It's definitely worth a laugh, but Travis Tritt made a good point in 1991: if you do the breaking up, don't expect sympathy when being single isn't as fun as it sounds.

"DON'T THINK I DON'T THINK ABOUT IT"
—DARIUS RUCKER

Darius Rucker's 2008 country debut was a lesson in wondering what could have been. If you cut and run, you'll never find out.

"How Do You Like Me Now?!" —Toby Keith

In 1999, Toby Keith knew the best way to get back at the ex who broke your heart is to grab hold of life and live it to the fullest.

"Let Me Let Go" —Faith Hill

Sometimes the hardest part of getting over a breakup is convincing yourself to move on, sang Faith Hill in 1998.

"You'll Think of Me" —Keith Urban

This No. 1 from 2004 found Keith Urban keeping his head held high, even after getting his heart tossed around.

chapter nine

HEALTHY LIVING,

country style

In the old days, healthy living meant loving through food and eating hearty for a demanding lifestyle. But as the modern world becomes more about convenience and less about elbow grease, attitudes are starting to change.

"I FEEL MUCH BETTER NOW AT THIRTY-THREE THAN I DID WHEN I WAS TWENTY, BECAUSE I TAKE BETTER CARE OF MYSELF."

Healthy as she is now, even Carrie Underwood remembers a time in her life when she had to change her ways.

THREE SQUARES

"I TRY TO GET SOME PROTEIN IN ME: YOGURT, OATMEAL, EGGS, OR SOME KIND OF PROTEIN SHAKE. I FIND THAT IT GIVES YOU MORE ENERGY IN THE MIDDLE OF THE DAY WHEN IT'S HARDEST FOR ME TO EAT BECAUSE I'M USUALLY PRETTY BUSY."

FRANKIE BALLARD

You don't have to be a nutritionist to know that breakfast is the most important meal, says Frankie Ballard.

TRICK PONY'S HEIDI NEWFIELD

"I HAVE FOUND THAT PREPARING MY FOODS FOR THE WHOLE WEEK IS REALLY, REALLY HELPFUL.... CHANCES ARE WHEN I COME IN, IF ALL I HAVE IS THIRTY MINUTES BETWEEN APPOINTMENTS, I'M GOING TO GRAB SOMETHING HEALTHY BECAUSE IT'S ALREADY MADE AND RIGHT THERE. IF YOUR BODY IS HAPPY AND HEALTHY, THAT'S GOING TO POUR OUT OF YOU IN WHATEVER YOU'RE DOING IN LIFE."

For singer Heidi Newfield, planning meals ahead of time is not so hard, but it makes a huge difference.

MIRANDA LAMBERT

"YOU GET TIRED OF ANY DIET. I'VE TRIED EVERYTHING. I JUST LITERALLY WOULD MAKE GRILLED CHICKEN BREAST, SWEET POTATO SALAD. THERE WAS NO MIRACLE."

It wasn't until she stopped looking for an easy way out that Miranda Lambert lost twenty pounds.

When Trisha Yearwood's mother was diagnosed with breast cancer and switched to a vegetarian diet, it helped her enjoy two more years with family.

"I BELIEVE HER DIET GAVE HER MORE TIME, AND QUALITY TIME. I REALLY STARTED TO THINK ABOUT WHAT I PUT INTO MY BODY."

TRISHA YEARWOOD

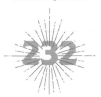

Tim McGraw has seen firsthand the benefits of switching to healthy habits, but he still makes sure not to be too hard on himself.

"ON TOUR, I TRY THREE TO FOUR DAYS A WEEK TO REALLY WATCH WHAT I EAT. BUT I LIKE CHEESEBURGERS, I LIKE PIZZA, I LIKE PASTA."

— TIM MCGRAW

"I LOVE THE WAY I FEEL WHEN I'M DONE. I KNOW I'VE ACCOMPLISHED SOMETHING AND I'M IN A GOOD MOOD THE REST OF THE DAY BECAUSE OF IT."

KENNY CHESNEY

Kenny Chesney, who works out regularly, might be one of the fittest men in country music, and he didn't get that way by accident.

"IT'S THE BEST THING YOU CAN DO FOR YOUR SANITY, NOT TO MENTION YOUR BODY. EXERCISE IS GOOD MEDICINE, SO FOLLOW YOUR BODY—IT WON'T LIE."

WILLIE NELSON

Take it from a man who has lived eighty-four years and counting: exercise can fix what ails you.

CARRIE
UNDERWOOD

"KEEP IT SIMPLE. I LIKE SQUATS, LUNGES. IF I GO FOR A JOG
AND I MEET UP WITH A GOOD HILL, I WILL LUNGE UP THE HILL
AND THAT WILL BURN THEM OUT. AND I LISTEN TO ANGRIER
MUSIC—DISTURBED OR AVENGED SEVENFOLD, OR KICK IT A
LITTLE OLD SCHOOL WITH MÖTLEY CRÜE."

Getting legs like Carrie Underwood isn't
voodoo—it's just blood-pumping tunes
and sweat.

MIRANDA LAMBERT

"I HATE RUNNING. LIKE, IN HUGE RED LETTERS: I HATE RUNNING. BUT IF I PUT ON BRITNEY [SPEARS], I CAN PICTURE BRITNEY'S BODY, AND I'M LIKE, 'OH! FASTER!'"

If you've never been the type of person who enjoys a tough workout, don't worry—you're not alone. Miranda Lambert pushes through by visualizing her end goal.

If Tim McGraw wants to keep doing his favorite things, he knows he'll have to put in extra effort.

"I'M FORTY-EIGHT YEARS OLD. I DON'T WANT TO NOT BE ABLE TO GO UP THERE AND DO A TWO-HOUR HIGH-ENERGY SHOW."

TIM McGRAW

FEEL THE BURN

Luke Bryan has figured out that his kids are also great personal trainers.

"MY THING IS TRYING TO GO SPEND SOME TIME OUTSIDE WITH MY SONS AND THROW A BALL IN THE YARD. BENDING OVER AND PICKING THEM UP, WRESTLING AROUND IN THE YARD IS A PRETTY GOOD WORKOUT."

LUKE BRYAN

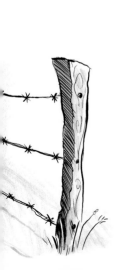

"I DON'T KNOW ANYBODY WHO IS BETTER DRUNK THANK SOBER. YOU MIGHT GET BY A WHILE, BUT SOONER OR LATER IT WILL TAKE YOU DOWN. I KNOW. I TRIED IT."

WILLIE NELSON

Willie Nelson might be known to enjoy a different kind of buzz, but before that his struggles with alcohol almost cost him his career—and his life.

"I GET OFF STAGE, JUST CHILL OUT, HAVE A COUPLE VODKA DRINKS. NOTHING TOO CRAZY. YOU START RUNNING OUT AND HITTING BARS AND TALKING OVER HOUSE BANDS, YOU'RE NOT GOING TO DO GOOD THE NEXT DAY."

Luke Bryan is often surrounded by people having the time of their lives, but he's learned that the party is often not worth the hangover.

JOHNNY CASH

"I KEPT HOPING THE PILLS I'D TAKEN WOULD BOOST ME UP TO WHERE I DIDN'T CARE ANYMORE, BUT THEY DIDN'T. IT WAS JUST A NIGHTMARE, AND I REMEMBER IT ALL WITH PERFECT CLARITY."

Like Johnny Cash at his disastrous 1962 performance at Carnegie Hall, an addict will likely need someone to be there offering support.

KEEP YOUR MIND RIGHT

BRANTLEY GILBERT

"YOU JUST NUMB THINGS OUT AND EVENTUALLY YOU START NUMBING ALL THE GOOD THINGS OUT. REALLY, I JUST WANTED TO MAXIMIZE AND ENJOY THE GOOD THINGS IN MY LIFE."

Brantley Gilbert lived hard every minute for many years, but then realized that endlessly looking for a good time was actually preventing them from happening.

When Lorrie Morgan actually thought about what she wanted from life, quitting smoking was a no-brainer.

"I QUIT SMOKING ABOUT TWELVE YEARS AGO, AND I WAS UP TO THREE PACKS A DAY. IT GOT TO THE POINT WHERE I COULD ONLY DO ONE SHOW, AND THEN I WAS DONE, COULDN'T TALK TO PEOPLE AFTER THE SHOW. AND ONE DAY I DECIDED THAT I WANTED TO SEE MY GRANDBABIES, AND I JUST QUIT SMOKING. IT WAS THE BEST THING I EVER DID."

LORRIE MORGAN

KEEP YOUR MIND RIGHT

Carrie Underwood's body gets way more attention than most, but she's learned to block out the pressure. She makes herself feel good and then loves that person.

"I HAVEN'T WEIGHED MYSELF IN A LONG TIME. IT'S MORE ABOUT BEING ABLE TO GO OUT ONSTAGE AND FEEL GOOD RUNNING AROUND."

CARRIE UNDERWOOD

"I'M NOT IN MY TWENTIES ANYMORE, AND THANK GOD—I COULDN'T LIVE THROUGH IT TWICE."

LORRIE MORGAN

To Lorrie Morgan, getting older isn't all bad. Wisdom comes with age!

"THE SECRET TO AGING GRACEFULLY? GOOD DOCTOR. GOOD LIGHTING. GOOD ATTITUDE. AND GOOD MAKEUP!"

DOLLY PARTON

Clearly, "good attitude" is the key among Dolly Parton's secrets to aging gracefully.

WILLIE NELSON

"THE BETTER WE TREAT OUR BODY, THE LONGER, HEALTHIER THE LIFE WE WILL HAVE, AND THE MORE WE WILL BE ABLE TO DO FOR THE WORLD AND OURSELVES."

According to Willie Nelson, staying healthy can do more than help us live longer, it can help give those lives more purpose.

MIRANDA LAMBERT

> "I'M SO EXCITED TO HEAD INTO MY THIRTIES, IT'S LIKE AN ADVENTURE. IT'S SOMETHING TO LOOK FORWARD TO AND HOPEFULLY GET SMARTER AND LEARN LESSONS FROM THE MISTAKES YOU'VE MADE. IT'S NOT A SCARY THING. IT'S EXCITING. WITH AGE YOU GAIN KNOWLEDGE, AND KNOWLEDGE IS BEAUTIFUL IN MY OPINION."

Some people might look back and imagine their best years are behind them, but not Miranda Lambert.

Carrie Underwood's
WORKOUT SECRETS

It's easy to get bored with working out or to be intimidated by the atmosphere at the gym—nobody wants to end up looking silly on the Internet for using a machine the wrong way. But Carrie Underwood has gotten into the best shape of her life by avoiding the gym altogether and using no special equipment, all while having fun.

Here's her secret workout, as she told *Self* magazine.

"I take a deck of cards and assign each suit a body area—say, diamonds for arms, hearts for legs, spades for core, and clubs for cardio," she explains. "I split the deck in half and write down exercises for each suit, a different one for each half. So, if I flip over the six of hearts, I'll do six squats. If the next card is ace of diamonds, that's fourteen push-ups. Sometimes I'll make spades boxing and beat the crap out of the bag for however many punches the number on the card says."

Underwood also keeps a joker in her deck to represent a one-mile run, then goes through the whole deck of cards. It takes her about an hour-and-a-half, but even if you've only got 20 minutes the principal is sound. By designing the workout yourself you're more likely to stick with it, and all the variety will keep you from losing interest. And best of all, you never have to leave home.

chapter ten

THE PEARLY

gates

Living so close to the natural way of things, the transition between Earth and Heaven is well known to country people and their stars. That doesn't make a loved one's passing any easier, but it does provide a sense of perspective and grace.

Joey Martin Feek of the husband-and-wife duo Joey & Rory passed away after a heroic battle with cancer at the age of forty in 2016.

"YOU HAVE A CHOICE OF WHETHER TO FACE THINGS AND HAVE A POSITIVE ATTITUDE OR A 'WOE IS ME' KIND OF ATTITUDE. WE GET TO GET UP EVERY DAY AND LIVE OUR BLESSINGS. IT'S BEEN HEAVY AT TIMES, BUT THE JOYS AND BLESSINGS OUT-WEIGH THE OTHER."

JOEY MARTIN FEEK

Since Joey Martin Feek passed away, her husband and singing partner Rory has realized that through him and the couple's daughter, Indiana, Joey's spirit will never truly die.

"I FELT HER PRESENCE THE WAY I DO MOST DAYS SINCE SHE'S BEEN GONE ... IN MY HEART, AND IN MY SOUL."

RORY FEEK

"I LOST CONSCIOUSNESS ABOUT FOUR TIMES AND WAS BROUGHT BACK. THAT'LL SCARE THE HELL OUT OF YOU. WE ALL THINK WE'RE INVINCIBLE UNTIL SOMETHING LIKE THAT HAPPENS. YOU NEVER KNOW WHEN YOUR LAST DAY WILL BE.... KELLY AND I WENT TO AUSTRALIA RECENTLY, AND I MIGHT NOT HAVE DONE THAT A FEW YEARS AGO. I WOULD HAVE SAID THAT IT'S TOO FAR OR I DIDN'T HAVE THE TIME. NOT ANYMORE. NOW, I GO AND DO WHAT MAKES ME HAPPY."

T.G. SHEPPARD

After emergency heart surgery, T.G. Sheppard found out that a more convenient time is not guaranteed to come.

WHAT TRULY MATTERS

"LOSING MY BROTHER CHANGED ME TREMEN-
DOUSLY AND LOSING [MY SISTER] KELLY, EVEN
MORE. I LITERALLY DO NOT TAKE ONE SECOND
FOR GRANTED."

LUKE
BRYAN

Both of Luke Bryan's siblings passed
away young and very suddenly. As a
result, he lives each day like it might
be his last.

RHONDA VINCENT

"I WAS TALKING TO THIS GIRL A COUPLE OF CHRISTMASES AGO. SHE WAS TELLING ME THAT HER FATHER HAD PASSED AWAY BUT SHE WAS UNABLE TO GET TO HIS FUNERAL BECAUSE SHE WAS SOMEWHERE OVERSEAS, AND I JUST THOUGHT TO MYSELF, 'HE'LL ALWAYS BE IN YOUR HEART, NO MATTER WHERE YOU ARE.'"

There's no substitute for the love a parent gives a child and according to bluegrass star Rhonda Vincent that love can extend beyond life itself.

GUY CLARK

"SOMETHING ELSE THAT'S IMPORTANT IS DIGNITY.... I'LL BET THAT WHEN YOU'RE DYING, YOU'RE NOT GOING TO THINK ABOUT THE MONEY YOU MADE. YOU'RE GOING TO THINK ABOUT YOUR ART."

Before he died in 2016 at the age of seventy-four, country legend Guy Clark figured out what matters most of all.

To Rory Feek of the duo Joey & Rory,
anything less than living life to its full
beauty would be to dishonor his wife, who
exemplified beauty even in tragic times.

"I WOULD LIKE TO THINK THAT LIFE CAN STILL GO ON AND STILL BE BEAUTIFUL IN SPITE OF THE FACT THAT JOEY IS NOT WITH US, AND IT IS. IT'S HARD, BUT IT'S STILL BEAUTIFUL."

RORY FEEK

THOSE WE LEAVE BEHIND

260

For Luke Bryan, coming to terms with the senselessness of death was perhaps the hardest part of losing his siblings.

"YOUR FAITH HAS TO GET YOU THROUGH ALL THAT. THAT'S NOT SAYING YOU DON'T QUESTION IT. BUT YOU JUST HAVE TO REVERT BACK TO YOUR FAITH IN GOD'S PLAN, THAT YOU'LL BE TOGETHER AGAIN AND THAT'S WHAT YOU HAVE TO GO ON."

LUKE BRYAN

"THERE'S A PICTURE OF ME AND MY DAD FROM WHEN I WAS A KID, AND HE'S PLAYING HIS GUITAR AND I'M LOOKING UP AT HIM. I HAVE THAT PHOTO OF HIM WITH ME, BECAUSE ALL THESE YEARS LATER, I'M DOING WHAT HE ALWAYS DREAMED OF DOING. IT GETS LONELY OUT HERE, AND IT'S COOL TO KNOW THAT I'M MAKING HIM PROUD."

COLE SWINDELL

Although Cole Swindell's father died in a tragic workshop accident, he takes comfort in the belief that his dad is still by his side.

THOSE WE LEAVE BEHIND

"I WATCHED AS MY MOTHER FELL TO HER KNEES AND LET HER HEAD DROP ONTO HER CHEST. MY POOR DADDY CAME UP TO HER AND TOOK HER ARM, BUT SHE BRUSHED HIM AWAY. 'I'LL GET UP WHEN GOD PUSHES ME UP!'"

JOHNNY CASH

Johnny Cash was just a boy when his brother Jack died, and he learned from his mother that the grieving process simply cannot be rushed.

TIM MCGRAW

> "HE GAVE ME SOMETHING THAT HE MIGHT NOT HAVE EVER KNOWN THAT HE GAVE ME. HE GAVE ME REASON TO THINK THAT I COULD MAKE SOMETHING OUT OF MY LIFE, BECAUSE HE DID. I DON'T KNOW THAT I WOULD HAVE HAD THE AMBITION TO DO THE THINGS THAT I'VE DONE WITHOUT THAT."

Tim McGraw didn't know his father, Major League Baseball pitcher Tug McGraw, until he was in his twenties, but they became close.

THOSE WE LEAVE BEHIND

CRAIG MORGAN

"THE LOSS OF OUR SON JERRY IS THE HARDEST THING WE HAVE EVER HAD TO ENDURE AS A FAMILY.... JERRY MAY BE GONE FROM THIS EARTH, AND WE WILL MISS HIM EVERY DAY, BUT HIS SPIRIT WILL LIVE ON IN OUR HEARTS. WE WILL FIND PEACE KNOWING THAT GOD HAS A BIGGER PLAN, AND THAT ONE DAY, WE'LL BE REUNITED WITH HIM AGAIN IN HEAVEN."

Craig Morgan's world came crashing down when his teenaged son died in a boating accident in 2016.

When Brad Paisley's hero and mentor Little Jimmy Dickens died, he found a new standard to live by.

"OUR PREACHER SAID, 'ALL OF YOU HERE TODAY SHOULD BE THINKING ABOUT YOUR OWN FUNERAL. BECAUSE IF YOU LIVE YOUR LIFE LIKE YOU'RE PLANNING THAT SHOW, YOUR LAST SHOW, THEN THAT'S A PRETTY GOOD WAY TO LIVE.'"

BRAD PAISLEY

He's hit the top of the country charts and lived out his dreams, but Craig Morgan hopes his biggest accomplishment will be the joy and happiness he brought to those around him.

"WHEN I'M NOT HERE ANYMORE, I HOPE THAT'S HOW PEOPLE WILL REMEMBER ME, WITH A SMILE ON MY FACE AND LOVING EVERY MINUTE OF MY LIFE, MY WIFE, MY KIDS, MY FAMILY, MY COUNTRY. AND HOPEFULLY, I WILL HAVE BEEN A POSITIVE INFLUENCE TO EVERYBODY."

CRAIG MORGAN

"IF YOUR ACTIONS CREATE A LEGACY THAT INSPIRES OTHERS TO DREAM MORE, LEARN MORE, DO MORE, AND BECOME MORE, THEN YOU ARE AN EXCELLENT LEADER."

By founding the Imagination Library, Dolly Parton is helping kids around the world learn to read.

268

"AT THE END OF THE DAY, YOUR LEGACY WILL
BE WHO YOU WERE."

Luke Bryan hopes he'll be remembered
not for his fame, but as a man who was
trustworthy, dedicated to faith, and a positive influence.

COUNTRY'S MOST UPLIFTING good-bye songs

"GO REST HIGH ON THAT MOUNTAIN"

Written by Vince Gill to honor the late Keith Whitley and Gill's brother Bob, "Go Rest High on That Mountain" captures the struggle to let a loved one go and eventually find peace.

"BELIEVE"

Released by Brooks & Dunn in 2005, "Believe" offers a path to solace for anyone dealing with a death in the form of advice passed down from a wise old neighbor.

"SEE YOU AGAIN"

In 2013, Carrie Underwood delivered a beautiful declaration of hope in the form of "See You Again," a faithful Top 5 hit about being reunited in Heaven.

"When I Get Where I'm Going"

This duet between Brad Paisley and Dolly Parton is a faithful reminder not to fear death, since believers are headed for a better place. It was a No. 1 hit in 2006.

"Live Like You Were Dying"

When Tim McGraw sings about a loved one learning his days are numbered, the urge to get up and start checking things off your bucket list is almost overwhelming.

"The Dance"

Immortalized by Garth Brooks, "The Dance" may be the best reminder to enjoy the ride of life ever written. Things will get messy, it says, but in the end it's a thing of true beauty.

afterword

After hearing it straight from the mouths of country music stars, it's clear that country wisdom comes in many forms. But whether it's wrapped in a timeless adage or just an off-the-cuff observation, there's one thing about the wisdom gained from a country life that's always the same—it's honest.

It's honest about dreams being the driving force behind almost everything, while reminding us that the chores still need to get done. It's honest about how love makes a person feel invincible, and also that hearts can shatter like glass. It doesn't lie when it tells us good times are balanced by their hangovers and bad times never last, and it aims for truth when it says family and legacy are all that matter in the end.

We let country stars deliver those messages in *The Little Book of Country Music Wisdom*, but they've probably helped you recall a few golden nuggets of your own—and you sure don't need a hit song to spread them around. Whether it's done over a tailgate or in an e-mail, it's a tradition that has endured for generations. Life is always throwing curveballs, after all, and you're never too old to need a little wisdom.

acknowledgments

Country stars are far from the only wise people in my life. I would like to thank those who have helped and encouraged me over the years, namely my amazing wife, Naomi; my mother, father, and stepparents, Suzanne, Tom, Jeff, and Candi; my brother Ben; the entire Parton, Fladie, and Heilmann families; and the Nashville music community—especially my mentors and earliest believers, Craig Shelburne and Calvin Gilbert.

sources

Chapter 1

1. Kacey Musgraves: *Nash Country Weekly*, July 6, 2015
2. Kelsea Ballerini: *Nash Country Weekly*, May 2, 2016
3. Keith Urban: *Nash Country Weekly*, January 18, 2016
4. Chris Janson: Chris Parton interview 10/26/15 for *Rolling Stone Country*
5. Dierks Bentley: http://www.rollingstone.com/music/news/dierks-bentley-on-new-album-black-ive-claimed-the-right-to-be-me-20160527
6. Chase Bryant: Chris Parton interview 6/28/16 for bio
7. Scotty McCreery: Chris Parton interview 4/14/16 for *Nash Country Weekly*
8. Mark Chesnutt: http://tasteofcountry.com/mark-chesnutt-song-that-made-george-jones-mad/
9. Loretta Lynn: Chris Parton interview 3/14/16 for *Nash Country Weekly*
10. Cam: Chris Parton interview 11/12/15 for *Nash Country Weekly*
11. Miranda Lambert: http://www.post-gazette.com/ae/music/2016/07/01/Miranda-Lambert-veers-off-Keeper-of-the-Flame-Tour-to-open-for-Chesney/stories/201606290024
12. Billy Joe Shaver: Chris Parton interview 6/13/12 for *CMT*
13. Tim McGraw: http://www.brainyquote.com/search_results.html?q=tim&mcgraw
14. Craig Morgan: http://www.rollingstone.com/music/videos/see-craig-morgan-croon-autobiographical-a-whole-lot-more-to-me-20160602
15. Mickey Guyton: *Nash Country Weekly*, January 11, 2016

16. Dolly Parton: *Nash Country Weekly*, December 14, 2015
17. Rosanne Cash: *Johnny Cash: The Life* by Robert Hilburn. Little, Brown & Co., 2013
18. Kacey Musgraves: *Nash Country Weekly*, July 6, 2015
19. Chely Wright: http://www.cbsnews.com/news/chely-wright-nashvilles-quietly-rejected-me/
20. Charley Pride: http://theboot.com/charley-pride-interview-2016/
21. Carrie Underwood: *US Weekly*, June 6, 2016
22. Cam: Chris Parton interview 11/16 for *Nash Country Weekly*
23. Florida Georgia Line: https://bmlgprep.net/audio-florida-georgia-line-isnt-concerned-about-their-place-in-country-music/
24. Jason Aldean: http://tasteofcountry.com/jason-aldean-twitter-haters/
25. Kenny Chesney: http://radio.com/2014/09/09/kenny-chesney-reclaims-his-soul-cover-story/
26. Dallas Davidson: *Nashville Songwriter: The Inside Stories Behind Country Music's Greatest Hits* by Jake Brown. BenBella Books Inc., 2004
27. Luke Bryan: http://www.onecountry.com/luke-bryan-fans-1724282017.html
28. Chase Bryant: Chris Parton interview 6/28/16 for bio

Chapter 2

1. Blake Shelton: http://www.mensjournal.com/magazine/blake-shelton-natural-born-hell-raiser-20130711
2. Joe Nichols: http://www.nashcountrydaily.com/2016/05/20/joe-nichols-gets-personal-about-his-sexy-single-undone-his-baby-girls-and-baseball/
3. Justin Moore: Chris Parton interview 2/1/16 for *Nash Country Weekly*
4. Dolly Parton: http://www.torontosun.com/2016/08/12/country-music-legend-dolly-parton-says-shes-just-getting-started

5. David Nail: Chris Parton interview 2016 for bio
6. Eric Church: http://www.countryweekly.com/vault/eric-church-my-carolina
7. Willie Nelson: *Roll Me Up and Smoke Me When I Die* by Willie Nelson. William Morrow Paperbacks, 2013
8. Kellie Pickler: Chris Parton interview 6/2/15 for *Rolling Stone Country*
9. Cole Swindell: http://parade.com/483493/rachelweingarten/country-star-cole-swindell-on-fathers-day-and-his-hit-single-you-should-be-here/
10. Dolly Parton: http://www.rollingstone.com/music/features/dolly-parton-on-greatest-gift-you-will-ever-know-the-ram-report-20160503
11. Kelsea Ballerini: *Nash Country Weekly*, May 2, 2016
12. Keith Urban: http://www.rollingstone.com/music/features/keith-urbans-hard-road-20160616?page=4
13. Brothers Osborne: Chris Parton interview 8/28/14 for *CMT*
14. Johnny Cash: *Johnny Cash: The Life*
15. Luke Bryan: http://www.rollingstone.com/music/features/luke-bryan-the-rolling-stone-country-interview-20150908?page=7
16. Jennifer Nettles: http://www.nashcountrydaily.com/2016/05/17/jennifer-nettles-charts-her-own-course-of-personal-exploration-with-fiery-new-album/
17. Thompson Square: http://spotlightnews.com/news/2016/07/06/the-darling-duo-of-country-music-thompson-square/
18. Willie Nelson: *Roll Me Up and Smoke Me When I Die*
19. Kenny Rogers: *Nash Country Weekly*, January 11, 2016
20. Tanya Tucker: Chris Parton interview 4/17/15 for *Nash Country Weekly*
21. Charles Kelley: Chris Parton interview 1/25/16 for *Nash Country Weekly*

22. Tim McGraw: http://www.eonline.com/news/651399/
tim-mcgraw-swears-he-s-not-that-tough-on-his-daughters-
boyfriends-but-what-about-faith-hill

Chapter 3

1. Tim McGraw: http://www.brainyquote.com/search_results.
html?q=tim&mcgraw
2. Reba McEntire: *Nash Country Weekly*, April 4, 2016
3. Tom T. Hall: *Nashville Songwriter*, 2014
4. Collin Raye: *Nash Country Weekly*, May 2, 2016
5. George Jones: http://www.cbn.com/cbnmusic/interviews/700club_
georgejones_060305.aspx?mobile=false&u=1
6. Kris Kristofferson: http://www.rollingstone.com/music/features/
kris-kristofferson-an-outlaw-at-80-20160606?page=2
7. Kelsea Ballerini: Country Weekly, May 25, 2015
8. Neal McCoy: http://www.adn.com/music/article/mr-nice-
guy-country-musics-neal-mccoy-success-follows-golden-
rule/2015/05/13/
9. Carrie Underwood: http://celebritybabies.people.com/2015/10/19/
carrie-underwood-son-isaiah-christian-people-cover/
10. Willie Nelson: *Roll Me Up and Smoke Me When I Die*
11. Johnny Cash: *Johnny Cash: The Life*
12. Willie Nelson: *Roll Me Up and Smoke Me When I Die*
13. Kenny Chesney: http://radio.com/2014/09/09/kenny-chesney-
reclaims-his-soul-cover-story/
14. Ty Herndon: http://www.people.com/article/ty-herndon-comes-
out-gay
15. Luke Bryan: http://qpolitical.com/luke-bryan-reveals-the-
tragedies-that-keep-his-faith-in-jesus-strong/
16. Wynonna: YouTube video: "I Can Only Imagine" from *Wynonna
Judd: Her Story—Scenes from a Lifetime* DVD, https://www.
youtube.com/watch?v=fxt5TsmEZaY
17. Johnny Cash Cave Story: *Johnny Cash: The Life*

Chapter 4

1. Charlie Daniels: *Growing Up Country: What Makes Country Life Country* by Charlie Daniels. Flying Dolphin Press/Broadway Books, 2007

2. Brandy Clark: http://www.rollingstone.com/music/news/brandy-clark-on-the-antiheroes-of-new-album-big-day-in-a-small-town-20160615?page=4

3. Kenny Chesney: http://radio.com/2014/09/09/kenny-chesney-reclaims-his-soul-cover-story/

4. Alan Jackson: http://www.people.com/people/archive/article/0,,20184693,00.html

5. Justin Moore: http://www.cmt.com/news/1622501/justin-moores-small-town-values-pay-off/

6. Loretta Lynn: https://www.brainyquote.com/quotes/quotes/l/lorettalyn313333.html

7. Jason Aldean: http://www.cmt.com/news/1767867/what-jason-aldean-learned-from-his-dad/

8. Billy Joe Shaver: Chris Parton interview 6/13/12 for *CMT*

9. Willie Nelson: *Roll Me Up and Smoke Me When I Die*

10. Miranda Lambert: http://www.redbookmag.com/life/interviews/a14751/miranda-lambert-interview-on-marriage-and-music/

11. Kip Moore: Chris Parton interview 3/7/16 for *Nash Country Weekly*

12. Trace Adkins: http://theboot.com/trace-adkins-toby-keith-tour-dates-2010/

13. Bill Anderson: *Nashville Songwriter*, 2014

14. Kellie Pickler: http://www.aarp.org/relationships/grandparenting/info-09-2009/kellie_pickler.html

15. Charlie Daniels: *Growing Up Country: What Makes Country Life Country*

16. Cam: Chris Parton interview 11/12/15 for *Nash Country Weekly*

17. Faith Hill: http://www.azquotes.com/quote/638309

18. Dan & Shay: http://theboot.com/dan-and-shay-from-the-ground-up/
19. Tim McGraw: http://www.brainyquote.com/quotes/quotes/t/timmcgraw363542.html
20. Kenny Rogers: http://www.nashcountrydaily.com/2016/05/20/kenny-rogers-kicks-off-final-tour-reveals-the-secret-to-great-chicken-talks-the-big-lebowski/
21. Kris Kristofferson: http://www.rollingstone.com/music/features/kris-kristofferson-an-outlaw-at-80-20160606?page=2
22. Loretta Lynn: http://www.brainyquote.com/quotes/authors/l/loretta_lynn.html
23. Willie Nelson: *Roll Me Up and Smoke Me When I Die*
24. Kellie Pickler: http://www.aarp.org/relationships/grandparenting/info-09-2009/kellie_pickler.html
25. Alabama: Chris Parton interview 9/3/15 for *Rolling Stone Country*
26. Tim McGraw: http://www.brainyquote.com/search_results.html?q=tim&mcgraw&pg=2
27. Rascal Flatts: http://www.cmt.com/news/1690654/offstage-rascal-flatts-share-deep-faith/
28. Lonestar: Chris Parton interview 4/20/16 for *Nash Country Weekly*
29. Willie Nelson: *Roll Me Up and Smoke Me When I Die*
30. Miranda Lambert: Miranda Lambert via Twitter

Chapter 5

1. Willie Nelson: *Roll Me Up and Smoke Me When I Die*
2. Jason Aldean: http://www.cmt.com/news/1767867/what-jason-aldean-learned-from-his-dad/
3. Kristian Bush: *Country Weekly*, May 25, 2015
4. Dustin Lynch: *Nash Country Weekly*, March 28, 2016
5. Justin Moore: Chris Parton 2/1/16 for *Nash Country Weekly*
6. Kenny Chesney: http://radio.com/2014/09/09/kenny-chesney-reclaims-his-soul-cover-story/
7. Reba McEntire: *Nash Country Weekly*, April 4, 2016

8. Frankie Ballard: *Nash Country Weekly*, November 9, 2015
9. Keith Urban: *Nash Country Weekly*, January 18, 2016
10. Johnny Cash: *Johnny Cash: The Life*
11. Randy Rogers Band: *Nash Country Weekly*, January 11, 2016
12. David Lee Murphy: *Nashville Songwriter*
13. Tim McGraw: http://www.nytimes.com/interactive/2015/09/30/fashion/mens-style/tim-mcgraws-grueling-workout.html
14. Chase Bryant: Chris Parton interview 6/28/16 for bio
15. Merle Haggard: *Nash Country Weekly*, April 25, 2016
16. Kenny Chesney: http://radio.com/2014/09/09/kenny-chesney-reclaims-his-soul-cover-story/
17. Carrie Underwood: Chris Parton interview 4/26/12 for *CMT*
18. Bill Anderson: *Nashville Songwriter*, 2014
19. Willie Nelson: *Roll Me Up and Smoke Me When I Die*
20. Tom T. Hall: *Nashville Songwriter*, 2014
21. Loretta Lynn: http://www.brainyquote.com/quotes/authors/l/loretta_lynn.html
22. Luke Bryan: http://www.rollingstone.com/music/features/luke-bryan-the-rolling-stone-country-interview-20150908?page=7
23. Randy Houser: *Nash Country Weekly*, March 28, 2016
24. John Rich: *Nashville Songwriter*
25. Old Dominion: Chris Parton interview 1/19/16 for *Nash Country Weekly*
26. Garth Brooks: http://www.brainyquote.com/search_results.html?q=garth&brooks
27. Tyler Farr: Chris Parton interview 3/15/16 for *Nash Country Weekly*
28. Luke Bryan: http://radio.com/2015/08/20/luke-bryan-kill-the-lights-spring-break-candle/
29. Kenny Chesney: http://radio.com/2014/09/09/kenny-chesney-reclaims-his-soul-cover-story/
30. Thomas Rhett: *Nash Country Weekly*, January 11, 2016

SOURCES

31. Lonestar: Chris Parton interview 4/20/16 for *Nash Country Weekly*

32. Kenny Rogers: *Nash Country Weekly*, January 11, 2016

Chapter 6

1. Kelsea Ballerini: *Nash Country Weekly*, May 2, 2016

2. Colt Ford: *Nash Country Weekly*, January 11, 2016

3. Tom T. Hall: *Nashville Songwriter*, 2014

4. Willie Nelson: *Roll Me Up and Smoke Me When I Die*

5. Randy Rogers Band: *Nash Country Weekly*, January 11, 2016

6. Lorrie Morgan—Chris Parton interview 1/12/16 for *Nash Country Weekly*

7. Luke Bryan: http://radio.com/2015/08/20/luke-bryan-kill-the-lights-spring-break-candle/

8. Willie Nelson: *Roll Me Up and Smoke Me When I Die*

9. Brad Paisley: *CMT* Hot 20 Countdown 3/13/15

10. Jason Aldean: http://tasteofcountry.com/jason-aldean-twitter-haters/

11. Jake Owen: Chris Parton interview 6/30/15 for *Rolling Stone Country*

12. Dallas Davidson: *Nashville Songwriter*, 2014

13. Luke Bryan: Chris Parton interview 5/21/16 for *Rolling Stone Country*

14. Cole Swindell: http://draftmag.com/cole-swindell-interview-tour/

15. Blake Shelton: http://www.mensjournal.com/magazine/blake-shelton-natural-born-hell-raiser-20130711

16. Miranda Lambert: http://www.womenshealthmag.com/weight-loss/miranda-lambert-weight-loss

17. Kip Moore: Chris Parton interview 3/7/16 for *Nash Country Weekly*

18. Brantley Gilbert: Chris Parton interview 3/21/14 for *CMT*

19. Willie Nelson: *Roll Me Up and Smoke Me When I Die*

Chapter 7

1. Dolly Parton: http://www.nytimes.com/2016/07/03/arts/music/dolly-parton-is-proud-of-her-gay-fans-and-hillary-clinton.html?_r=0

2. Brantley Gilbert: http://www.greenbaypressgazette.com/story/entertainment/music/2016/04/21/brantley-gilbert-talks-lambeau-his-harleys/83182262/

3. Johnny Cash: *Johnny Cash: The Life*

4. Blake Shelton: http://www.etonline.com/news/190083_blake_shelton_gushes_that_gwen_stefani_inspired_his_new_album_is_his_closest_ally/

5. Hunter Hayes: http://www.azquotes.com/quote/915123

6. Carrie Underwood: http://people.com/celebrity/carrie-underwood-im-horrible-around-guys/

7. Dierks Bentley: http://www.rollingstone.com/music/news/dierks-bentley-on-new-album-black-ive-claimed-the-right-to-be-me-20160527

8. Garth Brooks: http://www.reviewjournal.com/neon/sounds/garth-brooks-brings-the-charm-and-film-crews-back-the-strip

9. Kellie Pickler: *Nash Country Weekly*, July 6, 2015

10. Keith Urban: *Nash Country Weekly*, January 18, 2016

11. Miranda Lambert: http://www.cosmopolitan.com/entertainment/a50090/miranda-lambert-january-2016/

12. Carrie Underwood: http://people.com/celebrity/carrie-underwood-how-i-keep-my-marriage-to-mike-fisher-hot/

13. Dolly Parton: *Nash Country Weekly*, April 4, 2016

14. Kip Moore: Chris Parton interview 3/7/16 for *Nash Country Weekly*

15. Luke Bryan: http://www.womenshealthmag.com/life/luke-bryan

16. Alan Jackson: http://theboot.com/alan-jackson-denise-jackson-love-stories/

17. Josh Turner: http://www.eharmony.com/dating-advice/about-you/josh-turner-talks-man-stuff-and-marriage/#.WJzrx7YrJ-U

18. Carrie Underwood: http://people.com/celebrity/carrie-underwood-how-i-keep-my-marriage-to-mike-fisher-hot/

SOURCES

Chapter 8

1. Brandy Clark: https://www.theguardian.com/music/2016/jun/16/brandy-clark-country-music-nashville-interview
2. Willie Nelson: *Roll Me Up and Smoke Me When I Die*
3. Maren Morris: http://www.rollingstone.com/music/news/maren-morris-on-voice-rejection-hungover-inspiration-and-unruly-hero-20160616
4. Scotty McCreery: Chris Parton interview 4/14/16 for *Nash Country Weekly*
5. Luke Bryan: http://www.rollingstone.com/music/features/luke-bryan-the-rolling-stone-country-interview-20150908?page=7
6. Jason Aldean: http://www.cmt.com/news/1729999/jason-aldean-tells-haters-to-move-on/
7. Dierks Bentley: http://www.rollingstone.com/music/news/dierks-bentley-on-new-album-black-ive-claimed-the-right-to-be-me-20160527
8. Brandy Clark: https://www.theguardian.com/music/2016/jun/16/brandy-clark-country-music-nashville-interview
9. Willie Nelson: *Roll Me Up and Smoke Me When I Die*
10. Chris Young: Chris Parton interview 9/8/15 for *Nash Country Weekly*
11. Kip Moore: Chris Parton interview 3/7/16 for *Nash Country Weekly*
12. Loretta Lynn: http://www.brainyquote.com/quotes/authors/l/loretta_lynn.html
13. Miranda Lambert: http://www.cosmopolitan.com/entertainment/a50090/miranda-lambert-january-2016/
14. Willie Nelson: *Roll Me Up and Smoke Me When I Die*
15. Hunter Hayes: http://www.azquotes.com/quote/915123
16. Kristian Bush: *Country Weekly*, May 25, 2015
17. Lorrie Morgan: Chris Parton interview 1/12/16 for *Nash Country Weekly*
18. Reba McEntire: http://www.cmt.com/news/1763258/reba-the-divorce-was-not-my-idea/

Chapter 9

1. Carrie Underwood: *US Weekly*, June 6, 2016
2. Frankie Ballard: *Nash Country Weekly*, November 9, 2015
3. Heidi Newfield: *Nash Country Weekly*, January 18, 2016
4. Miranda Lambert: http://www.womenshealthmag.com/weight-loss/miranda-lambert-weight-loss
5. Trisha Yearwood: http://www.goodhousekeeping.com/life/inspirational-stories/interviews/a19856/trisha-yearwood/
6. Tim McGraw: http://www.nytimes.com/interactive/2015/09/30/fashion/mens-style/tim-mcgraws-grueling-workout.html
7. Kenny Chesney: http://www.menshealth.com/fitness/kenny-chesney-workout
8. Willie Nelson: *Roll Me Up and Smoke Me When I Die*
9. Carrie Underwood: *US Weekly*, June 6, 2016
10. Miranda Lambert: http://www.womenshealthmag.com/weight-loss/miranda-lambert-weight-loss
11. Tim McGraw: http://www.nytimes.com/interactive/2015/09/30/fashion/mens-style/tim-mcgraws-grueling-workout.html
12. Luke Bryan: http://www.womenshealthmag.com/life/luke-bryan
13. Willie Nelson: *Roll Me Up and Smoke Me When I Die*
14. Luke Bryan: http://www.rollingstone.com/music/features/luke-bryan-the-rolling-stone-country-interview-20150908?page=7
15. Johnny Cash: *Johnny Cash: The Life*
16. Brantley Gilbert: Chris Parton interview 3/21/14 for *CMT*
17. Lorrie Morgan: Chris Parton interview 1/12/16 for *Nash Country Weekly*
18. Carrie Underwood: *US Weekly*, June 6, 2016
19. Lorrie Morgan: Chris Parton interview 1/12/16 for *Nash Country Weekly*
20. Dolly Parton: http://buffalo.com/2016/06/07/news/music/concert-previews/dolly-parton-from-backwoods-barbie-to-country-queen/

21. Willie Nelson: *Roll Me Up and Smoke Me When I Die*
22. Miranda Lambert: http://radio.com/2014/06/06/interview-miranda-lambert-platinum/

Chapter 10

1. Joey Martin Feek: *Nash Country Weekly*, March 28, 2016
2. Rory Feek: This Life I Live blog 6/16/16
3. T.G. Sheppard. *Nash Country Weekly*, January 25, 2016
4. Luke Bryan: http://www.etonline.com/news/159231_luke_bryan_takes_in_his_13_year_old_nephew_following_his_brother_law_death/
5. Rhonda Vincent: *Nash Country Weekly*, December 14, 2015
6. Guy Clark: http://www.thetimes.co.uk/article/guy-clark-cf5k58fmb
7. Rory Feek: http://abcnews.go.com/Entertainment/rory-feek-retired-music-wife-joey-feeks-death/story?id=42010022
8. Luke Bryan: http://qpolitical.com/luke-bryan-reveals-the-tragedies-that-keep-his-faith-in-jesus-strong/
9. Cole Swindell: http://tasteofcountry.com/cole-swindell-winding-road-to-stardom/
10. Johnny Cash: *Johnny Cash: The Life*
11. Tim McGraw: http://www.huffingtonpost.com/2013/08/16/tim-mcgraw-dad-tug-pitcher_n_3768403.html
12. Craig Morgan: public statement via Facebook following death of son
13. Brad Paisley: http://tasteofcountry.com/brad-paisley-little-jimmy-dickens-legacy/
14. Craig Morgan: *Nash Country Weekly*, November 9, 2015
15. Dolly Parton: http://www.goodreads.com/quotes/39182-if-your-actions-create-a-legacy-that-inspires-others-to
16. Luke Bryan: http://www.rollingstone.com/music/features/luke-bryan-the-rolling-stone-country-interview-20150908?page=7

about the author

Chris Parton is a Nashville-based editor and journalist whose work has appeared in *Rolling Stone Country*, *Nash Country Weekly*, *CMT*, *Nashville Scene*, *Nashville Lifestyles*, *Native*, and *Taste of Country*. Since entering the music industry in 2007, he has interviewed hundreds of country artists—including many of those featured in *The Little Book of Country Music Wisdom*—gaining a unique insight into their stories and a genuine appreciation for the lessons they share.

about the illustrator

Noah Albrecht's illustrations have been used to promote major projects for film and TV such as *Star Wars*, *Lord of the Rings*, and NBC's hit show *Heroes*. Based in Nashville, Tennessee, he is a graduate of The Art Institute with a client list including Lucasfilm, New Line Cinema, and Universal Studios.